The Industrial Revolution in England

Random House Historical Issues Series

GENERAL EDITORS:

BRIAN TIERNEY

DONALD KAGAN

L. PEARCE WILLIAMS

CONSULTING EDITOR:

Eugene Rice

THE INDUSTRIAL REVOLUTION IN ENGLAND– BLESSING OR CURSE TO THE WORKING MAN?

Random House

Eleventh Printing

© *Copyright, 1967, by Random House, Inc.*

All rights reserved
under International and Pan-American Copyright Conventions.
Published in New York by Random House, Inc.,
and simultaneously in Toronto, Canada,
by Random House of Canada Limited.
Library of Congress Catalog Card Number: 68-13185
Manufactured in the United States of America
Printed and Bound by Edwards Brothers, Inc.,
Ann Arbor, Michigan

Preface

A major purpose of this series of pamphlets is to convince students in Western civilization courses that the essential task of a historian is not to collect dead facts but to confront live issues. The issues are alive because they arise out of the tensions that men have to face in every generation—tensions between freedom and authority, between reason and faith, between human free will and all the impersonal circumstances that help to shape our lives.

In order to achieve any sophisticated understanding of such matters, a student needs to read the views of great modern historians as they are set out in their own words. He needs to develop a measure of critical historical insight by comparing these often conflicting views with the source material on which they are based. He needs above all to concern himself with the great issues that have shaped the course of Western civilization and not with historical "problems" that are mere artificially contrived conundrums.

We believe that there are three major themes whose development and interplay have shaped the distinctive characteristics that set Western civilization apart from the other great historic cultures. They are the growth of a tradition of rational scientific inquiry, the persistence of a tension between Judaeo-Christian religious ideals and social realities, the emergence of constitutional forms of government. These three themes are introduced in the first pamphlets of the series. The reader will find them recurring in new forms and changing contexts throughout the rest of the pamphlets. We hope that in studying them he will come to a richer understanding of the heritage of Western civilization—and of the historian's approach to it.

Ithaca, 1968   BRIAN TIERNEY

                                  DONALD KAGAN

                                  L. PEARCE WILLIAMS

The Industrial Revolution in England—Blessing or Curse to the Working Man?

CONTENTS

QUESTIONS FOR STUDY

1   *What was the condition of the rural workers in the eighteenth century?*

2   *What were the essential changes required of a person when a shift was made
from the country to a manufacturing city?*

3   *What working conditions were detrimental to the children employed in
factories? What conditions might be beneficial?*

4   *What are the main points at issue between the Hammonds and Ashton?
Between Mantoux and Ashton?*

5   *By what criteria can a judgment be made on whether the Industrial Revolution
was a blessing or a curse to the working man?*

The very term "Industrial Revolution" brings to mind a violent upheaval and implies the drastic dislocation of a whole segment of society. The dice would thus seem to be loaded in favor of the view that, at least in the short run, it brought nothing but ill to those whose sweat made it possible. Yet it should not be forgotten that it took almost a century for the Industrial Revolution to occur—the standard dates are 1760–1830—and one wonders if "Revolution" is the proper term. Furthermore, there were other economic changes in this period that were both independent of, and supplementary to, the Industrial Revolution. British agriculture was changing rapidly and at some human cost. Would there have been less misery had the Industrial Revolution not been contemporary with the acceleration of the Enclosure movement? Or would there have been more? Is there, in fact, a "price" that must always be paid for industrialization, as so many people believe today when a nation must industrialize or die?

1 The Industrial Revolution Defined

The term "Industrial Revolution" was first given common currency in the lectures of Arnold Toynbee (1852–1883). It is in one of these lectures that he gave the classic definition of the fundamental economic changes that England had undergone in the years following 1750.

FROM *Lectures on the Industrial Revolution of the 18th Century in England* BY ARNOLD TOYNBEE

THE ESSENCE OF THE INDUSTRIAL REVOLUTION is the substitution of competition for the mediaeval regulations which had previously controlled the production and distribution of wealth. . . .

Coming to the facts of the Industrial Revolution, the first thing that strikes us is the far greater rapidity which marks the growth of population. Before 1751 the largest decennial increase, so far as we can calculate from our imperfect materials, was 3 per cent. For each of the next three decennial periods the increase was 6 per cent.; then between 1781 and 1791 it was 9 per cent.; between 1791 and 1801, 11 per cent.; between 1801 and 1811, 14 per cent.; between 1811 and 1821, 18 per cent. This is the highest figure ever reached in England, for since 1815 a vast emigration has been always tending to moderate it; between 1815 and 1880 over eight millions (including Irish) have left our shores. But for this our normal rate of increase would be 16 or 18 instead of 12 per cent. in every decade.

Next we notice the relative and positive decline in the agricultural population. In 1811 it constituted 35 per cent. of the whole population of Great Britain; in 1821, 33 per cent.; in 1831, 28 per cent. And at the same time its actual numbers have decreased. In 1831 there were 1,243,057 adult males employed in agriculture in Great Britain; in 1841 there were 1,207,989. In

Arnold Toynbee, *Lectures on the Industrial Revolution of the 18th Century in England* (1887), pp. 85, 87–93.

1851 the whole number of persons engaged in agriculture in England was 2,084,153; in 1861 it was 2,010,454, and in 1871 it was 1,657,138. Contemporaneously with this change, the centre of density of population has shifted from the Midlands to the North; there are at the present day 458 persons to the square mile in the countries north of the Trent, as against 312 south of the Trent. And we have lastly to remark the change in the relative population of England and Ireland. Of the total population of the three kingdoms, Ireland had in 1821 32 per cent., in 1881 only 14.6 per cent.

An agrarian revolution plays as large part in the great industrial change of the end of the eighteenth century as does the revolution in manufacturing industries, to which attention is more usually directed. Our next inquiry must therefore be: What were the agricultural changes which led to this noticeable decrease in the rural population? The three most effective causes were: the destruction of the common-field system of cultivation; the enclosure, on a large scale, of common and waste lands; and the consolidation of small farms into large. We have already seen that while between 1710 and 1760 some 300,000 acres were enclosed, between 1760 and 1843 nearly 7,000,000 underwent the same process. Closely connected with the enclosure system was the substitution of large for small farms. In the first half of the century Laurence, though approving of consolidation from an economic point of view, had thought that the odium attaching to an evicting landlord would operate as a strong check upon it. But these scruples had now disappeared. Eden in 1795 notices how constantly the change was effected, often accompanied by the conversion of arable to pasture; and relates how in a certain Dorsetshire village he found two farms where twenty years ago there had been thirty. The process went on uninterruptedly into the present century. Cobbett, writing in 1826, says: "In the parish of Burghclere one single farmer holds, under Lord Carnarvon, as one farm, the lands that those now living remember to have formed fourteen farms, bringing up in a respectable way fourteen families." The consolidation of farms reduced the number of farmers, while the enclosures drove the labourers off the land, as it became impossible for them to exist without their rights of pasturage for sheep and geese on common lands.

Severely, however, as these changes bore upon the rural population, they wrought, without doubt, distinct improvement from an agricultural point of view. They meant the substitution of scientific for unscientific culture. "It has been found," says Laurence, "by long experience, that common or open fields are great hindrances to the public good, and to the honest improvement which every one might make of his own." Enclosures brought an extension of arable cultivation and the tillage of inferior soils; and in small farms of 40 to 100 acres, where the land was exhausted by repeated corn crops, the farm buildings of clay and mud walls and three-fourths of the estate often saturated with water, consolidation into farms of 100 to 500 acres meant rotation of crops, leases of nineteen years, and good farm buildings. The period was one of great agricultural advance; the breed of cattle was improved, rotation of crops was generally introduced, the steam-plough was invented, agricultural societies were instituted. In one respect alone the change was injurious. In consequence of the high prices of corn which prevailed during the French war, some of the finest permanent pastures were broken up. Still, in spite of this, it was said in 1813 that during the previous ten years agricultural produce had increased by one-fourth, and this was an increase upon a great increase in the preceding generation.

Passing to manufactures, we find here the all-prominent fact to be the substitution of the factory for the domestic system, the consequence of the mechanical discoveries of the time. Four great inventions altered the character of the cotton manufacture; the spinning-jenny, patented by Hargreaves in 1770; the water-frame, invented by Arkwright the year before; Crompton's mule introduced in 1779, and the self-acting mule, first invented by Kelly in 1792, but not brought into use till Roberts improved it in 1825. None of these by themselves would have revolutionised the industry. But in 1769—the year in which Napoleon and Wellington were born—James Watt took out his patent for the steam-engine. Sixteen years later it was applied to the cotton manufacture. In 1785 Boulton and Watt made an engine for a cotton-mill at Papplewick in Notts, and in the same year Arkwright's patent expired. These two facts taken together mark the introduction of the factory system. But the most famous invention of all, and the most fatal to domestic industry, the power-loom, though also patented by Cartwright in 1785, did not come into use for several years, and till the power-loom was introduced the workman was hardly injured. At first, in fact, machinery raised the wages of spinners and weavers owing to the great prosperity it brought to the trade. In fifteen years the cotton trade trebled itself; from 1788 to 1803 has been called "its golden age;" for, before the power-loom but after the introduction of the mule and other mechanical improvements by which for the first time yarn sufficiently fine for muslin and a variety of other fabrics was spun, the demands became such that "old barns, cart-houses, out-buildings of all descriptions were repaired, windows broke through the old blank walls, and all fitted up for loom-shops; new weavers' cottages with loom-shops arose in every direction, every family bringing home weekly from 40 to 120 shillings per week." At a later date, the condition of the workman was very different. Meanwhile, the iron industry had been equally revolutionised by the invention of smelting by pit-coal brought into use between 1740 and 1750, and by the application in 1788 of the steam-engine to blast furnaces. In the eight years which followed this latter date, the amount of iron manufactured nearly doubled itself.

A further growth of the factory system took place independent of machinery, and owed its origin to the expansion of trade, an expansion which was itself due to the great advance made at this time in the means of communication. The canal system was being rapidly developed throughout the country. In 1777 the Grand Trunk canal, 96 miles in length, connecting the Trent and Mersey, was finished; Hull and Liverpool were connected by one canal while another connected them both with Bristol; and in 1792, the Grand Junction canal, 90 miles in length, made a waterway from London through Oxford to the chief midland towns. Some years afterwards, the roads were greatly improved under Telford and Macadam; between 1818 and 1829 more than a thousand additional miles of turnpike road were constructed; and the next year, 1830, saw the opening of the first railroad. These improved means of communication caused an extraordinary increase in commerce, and to secure a sufficient supply of goods it became the interest of the merchants to collect weavers around them in great numbers, to get looms together in a workshop, and to give out the warp themselves to the workpeople. To these latter this system meant a change from independence to dependence; at the beginning of the century the report of a committee asserts that the essential difference between the domestic and the factory system is, that in the latter the work is done "by persons who have no property in the goods they manufacture." Another direct consequence of this expansion of trade was the regular recurrence of periods of over-production and of depression, a phenomenon quite unknown under the old system, and due to this new form of production on a large scale for a distant market.

These altered conditions in the production of wealth necessarily involved an equal revolution in its distribution. In agriculture the prominent fact is an enormous rise in rents. Up to 1795, though they had risen in some places, in others they had been stationary since the Revolution. But between 1790 and 1833, according to Porter, they at least doubled. In Scotland, the rental of land, which in 1795 had amounted to £2,000,000, had risen in 1815 to £5,278,685. A farm in Essex, which before 1793 had been rented at 10s. an acre, was let in 1812 at 50s., though, six years after, this had fallen again to 35s. In Berks and Wilts, farms which in 1790 were let at 14s., were let in 1810 at 70s., and in 1820 at 50s. Much of this rise, doubtless, was due to money invested in improvements—the first Lord Leicester is said to have expended £400,000 on his property—but it was far more largely the effect of the enclosure system, of the consolidation of farms, and of the high price of corn during the French war. Whatever may have been its causes, however, it represented a great social revolution, a change in the balance of political power and in the relative position of classes. The farmers shared in the prosperity of the landlords; for many of them held their farms under beneficial leases, and made large profits by them. In consequence, their character completely changed; they ceased to work and live with their labourers, and became a distinct class. The high prices of the war time thoroughly demoralised them, for their wealth then increased so fast, that they were at a loss what to do with it. Cobbett has described the change in their habits, the new food and furniture, the luxury and drinking, which were the consequences of more money coming into their hands than they knew how to spend. Meanwhile, the effect of all these agrarian changes upon the condition of the labourer was an exactly opposite and most disastrous one. He felt all the burden of high prices, while his wages were steadily falling, and he had lost his common-rights. It is from this period, viz., the beginning of the present century, that the alienation between farmer and labourer may be dated.

Exactly analogous phenomena appeared in the manufacturing world. The new class of great capitalist employers made enormous fortunes, they took little or no part personally in the work of their factories, their hundreds of workmen were individually unknown to them; and as a consequence, the old relations between masters and men disappeared, and a "cash nexus" was substituted for the human tie. The workmen on their side resorted to combination, and Trades-Unions began a fight which looked as if it were between mortal enemies rather than joint producers. The misery which came upon large sections of the working people at this epoch was often, though not always, due to a fall in wages, for, as I said above, in some industries they rose. But they suffered likewise from the conditions of labour under the factory system, from the rise of prices, especially from the high price of bread before the repeal of the corn-laws, and from those sudden fluctuations of trade, which, ever since production has been on a large scale, have exposed them to recurrent periods of bitter distress. The effects of the Industrial Revolution prove that free competition may produce wealth without producing wellbeing. We all know the horrors that ensued in England before it was restrained by legislation and combination.

2   The World That Was Lost

Arthur Young (1741–1820) was a prosperous farmer who devoted his life to the improvement of agriculture. He traveled widely, keeping a journal in which he noted the condition of the countryside and reporting what he saw in the journal, Annals of Agriculture, *or in separate publications. These reports give an excellent insight into the conditions of Great Britain just as she plunged into the Industrial Revolution.*

In the first document, Young provides figures for the amount of capital required to set up as a farmer, leasing enough land to bring in an annual income of 100 pounds a year. Then he gives indications of the standard of living of cottagers (the poorest farmers).

FROM *Tours in England and Wales*

BY ARTHUR YOUNG

To Hire a Farm of 100l. a Year.

	£.		
5 Horses at 15l.	75	0	0
12 Cows at 7l.	84	0	0
8 Young cattle 3l.	24	0	0
60 Sheep at 10s.	30	0	0
2 Sows at 50s.	5	0	0
1 Waggon,	25	0	0
2 Tunbrils 10l.	20	0	0
1 Harvest cart,	7	0	0
2 Ploughs,	3	0	0

Arthur Young, *Tours in England and Wales selected from the Annals of Agriculture* (1932), pp. 1, 2–3, 5, 9, 45, 47–9, 87–90, 145, 157–8, 205, 217, 223–4, 274–5. Reprinted by permission of The London School of Economics and Political Science, London.

2 Harrows,	*3*	*0*	*0*
1 Roller,	*1*	*0*	*0*
Harness,	*5*	*0*	*0*
Sundries,	*15*	*0*	*0*
Furniture,	*50*	*0*	*0*
Tythe,	*12*	*0*	*0*
Rates, &c.	*5*	*0*	*0*
Housekeeping,	*25*	*0*	*0*
2 Men and 1 boy,	*19*	*0*	*0*
2 Maids,	*6*	*0*	*0*
1 Labourer,	*18*	*0*	*0*
60 Acres seed 12s.	*36*	*0*	*0*
	468	*0*	*0*

Land sells at 30 years purchase, in 10 years risen much, now at a stand. Land-tax at 4s. not more than 1s. the county through. Tythes not much gathered; computed 2s. to 3s. in the pound. Poor rates, 1s. to 1s. 6d. doubled in 10 years. Tea general, leases 7s. to 14s. or 21s. many, but going out.

Labour

In harvest 1s. 4d. 1s. 6d. and board
—Hay 1s. 2d. 1s. 4d. and beer.
—Winter 1s.
Man's wages 8l.
Lad 3l.
Maid 3l. to 3l. 10s.
Woman at hay 6d. and beer.

Rise of labour, none for 6 years, but in 15 years ⅓d

Provision

Cheese 3d.

Butter 6d. 9d.

Beef 4d.

Bacon 6d. 7d.

Potatoes 1s. 6d. 2s. strike,

Labourer's house rent 40s.

Mutton 4d.

Veal 4d.

Pork 4d.

Firing, seldom buy more
    than 12s. for 1 stack coal.

Tools 5s.

Building

Bricks 15s. formerly 9s.

Tiles 20s.

Oak 40s. a ton, very little advanced.

Ash do.

Poplar 30s.

Carpenter 1s. 6d. 1s. 8d.

Mason do.

Building a cottage 25l.

A Farm

300	Acres	8	Horses
124	Grass	16	Cows
176	Arable	4	Fatting
33	Wheat	30	Young
50	Barley	100	Sheep
8	Oats	3	Men
17	Pease	2	Maids
60	Clover	2	Labourers
8	Fallow		

*   *   *

The state of the poor, in general, in this country is advantageous, owing very much to lace making. The following account will shew this, in the receipt and expenditure of a poor family, viz. a man, his wife, and five children, the eldest sixteen years of age.

Earnings

	£.	s.	d.
Twenty-six weeks winter, at 7s. raised to that rate by taking work by the great	9	2	0
Five harvest, at 9s.	2	5	0
Four week's hay, going upwards (towards London)	3	3	0
Seventeen weeks summer, at 8s.	6	16	0
The son 3s. a week, and 16s. extra in hay and harvest	8	12	0
The rest of the family, 2s. a week	5	4	0
	35	2	0

Expenses

	£.	s.	d.
Bread, half the year (winter), barley, and half wheaten, at 6s. 6d. a week, on an average including baking, 4d. barm, 2d. and salt, 1d.	0	6	6
Salt for other uses,	0	0	0½
Bacon, 2 lb. a week	0	1	4
Tea, sugar, and butter	0	1	0
Cheese, half a pound	0	0	2½
Beer (four bushel of malt, at 5s. 6d. and 3 lb. hops, 3s.) per week	0	0	6
Soap (half a pound in three weeks), and starch, and blue	0	0	2
Candles	0	0	3
Thread, half an ounce a week, 1½d. worsted, 2d.	0	0	3½
	0	10	3¼
Per annum	26	15	2
Rent	1	15	0
Wood	0	12	0
Lying in and sickness	1	0	0

Cloaths. The man's shoes	0	15	0
shirts	0	8	0
stockings	0	4	0
hat, &c.	0	1	6
jacket	0	6	0
	1	14	6
Family	2	0	0

	£.	s.	d.
	3	14	6
	33	16	8
Earnings	35	2	0
Expenses	33	16	8
To lay up, or expend in additional cloaths	1	5	4

In the selections that follow, Young describes the conditions of rural life in a number of places throughout England and Wales.

OCTOBER 23, 1776, landed at Milford haven from Ireland. The whole country is inclosed, without such a thing as a common field. The food of the poor, bread and cheese, with broth made of salt meat, paid in at the cheapest season; much fish also eaten by them. Many keep cows; no goats on the mountains. The cottages many of them not a whit better than Irish cabbins, without an equal show of pigs, poultry and cows. Labour 8d. in the winter, and 10d. in summer, the year round. The whole country is in gentle inequalities; and, if wooded would be beautiful.

To Narbarth. Several cottages building in the Irish way, of mud with straw. The poor people seem well cloathed and fed. They use through all this country small heavy carts with two oxen and two or three horses, the driver sits on the front of the cart, and drives with reins.

October 24th to St. Clear. From Narbarth to Hubberston the course is, Rents 7s. 6d. to 10s. the whole farm through; to 14s. on some farms. Farms rise to very large ones, but in general small. The Irish cottar system is found here—3 or 4 cottages to a farm of 40 or 50l. a year. They are always at the call of the farmers, they are allowed two or three grass fields at a moderate rent, a cow or two, but no pigs, unless one in a year, to kill at Christmas. Strangers get in winter 4d. a day, and food; without food 8d. in harvest 1s. 1s. 6d. and food. They live on bread and cheese, and milk, or water; no beer, nor meat, except on a Sunday. The culture of potatoes increases much, more planted last year than ever known before. The poor eat them; and every cabbin has a garden with some in it. Many iron furnaces, the ore dug in the country. The poor people spin a good deal of wool, and weave it into flannel for their own wear, no linen is worn by them, flannel supplying the place. Query, to the physicians of the country—Is the rheumatism known here as much as in other countries where linen is worn? They make cloth also for their own wear. Weavers earn 1s. a day, and sometimes more. The poor live on barley-bread, cheese, and butter; not one in ten have either cows or pigs, fare very poorly and rarely touch meat. Their little gardens they plant with cabbages, carrots, leeks, and potatoes. Rent of a cottage and garden, 10s. to 20s. Building a mud cabbin costs 10l.

*   *   *

The Earl of Shelburne, though his attention has not been particularly applied to husbandry, yet having kept large tracts of land in his own hands and with very liberal views, his Lordship has planned a system of conduct which cannot fail of having excellent effects upon the husbandry of his extensive estate, and the neighbourhood in general. . . . It is his idea, that a man of large fortune keeping land in his hands with a view only of uniting the profits of the landlord and the farmer, is acting from very poor motives: That he ought to apply to farming either as a mere amusement, or which is better, as a means in which he can be of very great service to the country.

That in the first place he should have his grounds to exhibit to his tenants and others, cultivated in the most masterly manner which the climate and soil will admit of; that they may at all times see the culture of all those new plants which are recommended to farmers from the fields of gentlemen, that seeing the produce, the application, and the effect, they may, by degrees, be induced to make experiments themselves, and choose between objects, once equally unknown to them. That they may see the plants, to which they have always been accustomed, carried to the highest degree of perfection, by new successions of arrangement, new modes of culture and new exertions in manuring. From fields thus managed a farmer must always return wiser than he came.

In another line, who, says his Lordship, should introduce improvements in the breed of cattle and sheep; in the implements of husbandry; and in various other circumstances? the farmer, who, probably, sees little beyond what he has used and to whom a failure in success would be a heavy loss, or the landlord, who must necessarily have opportunities of seeing such variation and their effects, and to whom losses are an insignificant object?

Before I quit this country, I may remark, that I was much struck all through it, to find the Lombardy poplar so generally introduced; there is scarcely a house without some, and many of them very finely grown. But the cause to which this and other circumstances may be referred, is an article that escaped me when I was here before. It is, there being a great number of landlords the occupiers of their own lands. Alderton especially, is full of them; gentlemen farmers from 200 to 500l. a-year, who cultivating their own property, do it with a spirit that very few leases will permit. Within a very few years there are a great number of well-built brick houses, with inclosed and well-managed gardens; many new cottages; much planting; which, added to the excellent husbandry in the fields, give a beautiful appearance to the country, and prove, beyond a million of arguments, the admirable effects which flow from a wealthy yeomanry; a race of men so greatly decreased in this kingdom; and is a strong confirmation of what I have more than once remarked, that it is not the union of little farms we should complain of, but the accumulation of little estates, which, when they happen to be cultivated by their owners, promote, beyond any thing else, the prosperity of the national agriculture.

All this country abounds greatly in game, especially pheasants, which are so plentiful, that every little copse is full of them. At Boyton Mr. Woolnough, when I was here before, had them in his garden, and in severe weather they come to the corn stacks: besides a general plenty of game the country abounds greatly with the best sorts of fresh water fish; there is not a pond, or scarcely a large dyke at Alderton, Hollesley, Shottisham, or Bawdsey, that has not good carp and tench; carp rise to eight pound each, tench four pound, perch two pounds; and there are several fresh water creeks that communicate with the sea, in which they abound of the largest size; when to this we add wild fowl in plenty, a dry sandy but fertile soil, and the sea contiguous almost to every parish, it will not be doubted that few parts of the kingdom possess so many circumstances to make a residence in every respect plentiful, and in most agreeable. I know but one drawback; in the spots near the marshes they are plagued with agues, but the high sandy situations are free from them. Those marshes are narrow tracts on the river.

Next we went to Capel St. Andrews. Mr. Gross's great farm of 2700 acres, of whom, repeating our enquiries, we found, that he had been accustomed to cultivate carrots, even to last year, but his crops were so eaten up by the innumerable number of hares which his landlord, Lord Archibald Hamilton, preserved, that he has determined to sow no more. In these cases the tenant doubtless has his recompense in the rent, but the public has none. The profusion of game in this and another of his lordship's farms, Butley Abbey, Mr. Chandler's, which are together above 5000 acres, puts a barrier to good husbandry, and prevents one of the best articles of culture in the kingdom from spreading. It is not only the hares that do the mischief, but their preservation nurses up a breed of rabbits which add to the evil. The reflection I have added is my own, and not the farmer's, who seemed very well inclined to second his landlord's wishes.

*   *   *

Crossed the Severn at the ferry at Lincoln Hill, in the midst of a most noble scenery of exceeding bold mountainous tracts, with that river rolling at the bottom. The opposite shore is one immense steep of hanging wood, which has the finest effect imaginable. Mounted through that wood, thickly scattered with cottages, the inhabitants busily employed in the vast works of various kinds carried on in the neighbourhood. One circumstance I remarked which gave me much pleasure. There was not a single cottage in which a fine hog did not seem to make a part of every family; not a door without a stone trough with the pig eating his supper, in company with the children at the same business playful about the threshold. It was a sight which shewed that chearfulness and plenty crowned the board of the humble but happy inhabitants of this romantic spot.

About St. Neot's a vast improvement by an inclosure, which took place 16 years ago, which makes the country much more beautiful, and has been a great benefit to the community. A gentleman of the town however complained, as I rode thither with him, that, notwithstanding the productiveness of the soil was certainly greater, yet that the poor were ill-treated by having about half a rood given them in lieu of a *cow keep,* the inclosure of which land costing more than they could afford, they sold the lots at 5l. the money was drank out at the ale-house, and the men, spoiled by the habit, came, with their families, to the parish; by which means poor rates had risen from 2s. 6d. to 3s. and 3s. 6d. But pray, sir, have not rates arisen equally in other parishes, where no inclosure has taken place? Admitted. And what can be the good of commons, which would not prevent poor rates coming to such a height? Better modes of giving the poor a share might easily, and have been, as in other cases, adopted.

*   *   *

In the open fields the farms are generally small, usually about 70l. a-year: these little occupations with which the Duke of Grafton, and other good landlords have patience in order to nurse up industrious families, are yet a heavy loss in repairs: and sometimes in other circumstances: inclosed farms rise to 300l. which is the greatest; there are but few of 200l. to 250l. In farms of a tolerable size, the tenantry are substantial, and it gave me great pleasure to find them with such confidence in their landlord, as to raise considerable erections on the Duke's farms at their own expence, in articles beyond the common demands of the country; as a hay barn, &c. &c. and this while tenants at will; a sure proof that they regard their landlord as their father and their friend.

The 7th. To Measham, where Mr. Wilkes shewed us his many and great improvements; the manor and estate he purchased some years ago of Mr. Wollaston, of Finborough, in Suffolk, for 50,000l. The buildings erected and erecting will speedily change the face of it. Here are two cotton and a corn mill, two steam engines; many weaving-shops, and a number of cottages built; a large and handsome inn; . . . a few of the old thatched hovels remain to shew what this place was; what it will be may easily be conceived. But what is done here in ten or a dozen years by one man, who has been at the same time engaged in many other great undertakings, who, in union with Mr. Peele, is giving a new face to Faseley and Tamworth, cannot but make any one from the Continent admire at the wonderful exertions active in this kingdom—and in this kingdom only, for there is nothing out of it in the manufacturing world that is not, comparatively speaking, fast asleep.

A manufacturing town—Birmingham in the 1790s.

These immense works, which wear so animated a face of business, correspond well with the prodigious increase of the town, which I viewed to good advantage from the top of the new church of St. Paul: it is now a very great city indeed; and it was abundantly curious to have it pointed out to me the parts added since I was here. They form the greatest part of the town, and carry in their countenance undoubted marks of their modern date. In

1768 the population was under 30,000; now the common calculation is 70,000, but more accurate calculation extend it to 80,000, which I am told is the number assigned by Dr. Priestley. In the last 10 years above 4000 new houses have been built: and the increase is at present going on much more rapidly, for I was told that the number this year is not less than 700.

The earnings of the workmen in the manufacture are various, but in general very high: a boy of 10 or 12 years, 2s. 6d. to 3s. a week; a woman from 4s. to 20s. a week, average about 6s.; men from 10s. to 25s. a week, and some much higher; colliers earn yet more. These are immense wages, when it is considered that the whole family is sure of constant steady employment; indeed they are so great, that I am inclined to think labour higher at Birmingham than in any place in Europe: a most curious circumstance for the politician to reflect on, and which shews of how little effect to manufactures is cheap labour, for here is the most flourishing fabric that was perhaps ever known, paying the highest rates of labour. Such an instance ought to correct those common notions that have been retailed from hand to hand a thousand times, that cheap provisions are necessary for the good of manufactures, because cheap provisions suppose cheap labour, which is a combination founded in ignorance and error. Provisions at Birmingham are at the same rate as every where else in England, for it is remarkable that the level of price at present is very general, except the division of the east and west of the kingdom for corn; but while Birmingham and Norwich eat their provisions at nearly the same price (with allowance that the former is much the more quick, ready, and active market), the price of labour is at least 150 per cent. higher in one of those places than the other. Why then I enquire, what has provisions to do with the rate of labour? If one was to form our ideas from a very enlarged view of all the great fabrics in Europe, we should be apt to think that a great and flourishing fabric could not subsist, either with cheap provisions, or with cheap labour.

I tried hard to pick up some data, on which to calculate the amount of the fabric, but difficulties of various kinds prevented any accuracy in the estimation. In conversation with a very ingenious gentleman, who has written an able work on the town, and who was rewarded for it by having his house burnt down in the late riots, I mean Mr. Hutton, he informed me that ten years ago there were many estimates made with a good deal of care; and that on multiplied experiments it was found, that the returns per week, was equal to the rent per annum; including all the houses of the town on an average; all shops; all trades: the houses were then about 9000, and the rent 9l. each, on a medium; now the houses are about 13,000, and as I find, on enquiry, that the little houses, which have been built in such numbers for manufacturers, are let at 6l. 10s. the lowest; 7l. and 8l. each; 9l. on a general average of rents must now be much too low; however let us call it no more than 10l. this would make the rental of the town 130,000l. a year, and the returns of all its trade 6,760,000l. per annum: out of which a very great deduction is to be made for all the trades and professions of common life, supported by the manufacture, but not composing it. If I should form any idea corrective of this, it would be that the estimate is carried too high: let us suppose the population 80,000, then there are about 40,000 males, of these deduct 5000 not employed in the manufacture, remain 35,000; three-fourths of that number are of an age to be employed, or 26,250. Suppose these to earn, including manufacturers and merchants profit, 15s. a week, it amounts to 1,023,724l. a year. Of the 40,000 women 20,000 may be supposed to be employed, and to earn 6s. including, as above; the year's earnings will be 312,000l. in all 1,335,000l. double this, to include all raw materials, and you have 2,670,000l. for the amount of the manufacture. Now I am ready to grant, that here is a great deal of supposition in this estimate, but at the same time it is not altogether without data; and though the total may exceed this, possibly half a million, yet I think as much might be said to shew the calculation high, as to prove it low. It is true the ratio of the earnings is taken rather low, including, as it ought to do, the profit both of the manufacturer and of the merchant, which cannot well be less than 20 per cent.; but then the number of the workmen can scarcely exceed the supposition, probably not equal to it, 20,000 females, in particular are a high allowance.

Robert Southey (1774–1843) was Poet Laureate of England and intimately connected with the Romantic school of William Wordsworth and Samuel Taylor Coleridge. The Romantics tended to idealize the rural life and see in it a purity and simplicity that often was invisible to their contemporaries.

The selection that follows takes the form of a dialogue between Sir Thomas More's ghost and a man who speaks for Southey's time.

FROM *Sir Thomas More* BY ROBERT SOUTHEY

SIR THOMAS MORE. . . . The spirit which built and endowed monasteries is gone. Are you one of those persons who think it has been superseded for the better by that which erects steam-engines and cotton mills?

MONTESINOS. They are indeed miserable politicians who mistake wealth for welfare in their estimate of national prosperity; and none have committed this great error more egregiously than some of those who have been called statesmen by the courtesy of England. Yet the manufacturing system

Robert Southey, *Sir Thomas More; or, Colloquies on the Progress and Prospects of Society,* I (1829), 158–9, 166–7, 170–1, 173–4.

is a necessary stage in the progress of society. Without it this nation could not have supported the long and tremendous conflict which has delivered Europe from the yoke of military despotism, . . . the worst of all evils. If England had not been enabled by the use of steam-engines to send out every year myriads of brave men, and millions of specie, . . . what had Europe, and what had England itself been now? This inestimable benefit we have seen and felt. And from the consequences of that skill in machinery which the manufacturing system alone could have produced, we may expect ultimately to obtain the greatest advantages of science and civilization at the least expense of human labour.

* * *

SIR THOMAS MORE. There is an example before our eyes. Yonder children are on the way to a manufactory, where they pass six days out of the seven, from morning till night. Is it likely that the little they learn at school on the seventh (which ought to be their day of recreation as well as rest); should counteract the effects of such an education, when the moral atmosphere wherein they live and move and have their being, is as noxious to the soul, as the foul and tainted air which they inhale is to their bodily constitution?

MONTESINOS. Yet the most celebrated minister of the age, the only minister who for many generations has deserved to be called a Premier, the minister whom our best and wisest statesmen at this day profess entirely to admire and implicitly to follow, . . . he made his boast of this very evil, and congratulated Parliament that the nation had a new source of wealth and revenue in the labour of children: so completely had the political system in which he was trained up seared his heart and obscured his understanding.

SIR THOMAS MORE. Confess that this is an evil which had no existence in former times! There are new things under the sun, . . . new miseries, . . . new enormities, . . . this portentous age produces them.

* * *

SIR THOMAS MORE. What then shall we say of a system which in its direct consequences debases all who are engaged in it? a system that employs men unremittingly in pursuits unwholesome for the body, and unprofitable for the mind, . . . a system in which the means are so bad, that any result would be dearly purchased at such an expense of human misery and degradation, and the end so fearful, that the worst calamities which society has hitherto endured may be deemed light in comparison with it?

MONTESINOS. Like the whole fabric of our society it has been the growth of circumstances, not a system foreplanned, foreseen and deliberately chosen. Such as it is we have inherited it, . . . or rather have fallen into it, and must get out of it as well as we can. We must do our best to remove its evils, and to mitigate them while they last, and to modify and reduce it till only so much remains as is indispensable for the general good.

SIR THOMAS MORE. The facts will not warrant you in saying that it has come upon the country unsought and unforeseen. You have prided yourselves upon this system, you have used every means for extending it; you have made it the measure of your national prosperity. It is a wen, a fungous excrescence from the body politic: the growth might have been checked if the consequences had been apprehended in time; but now it has acquired so great a bulk, its nerves have branched so widely, and the vessels of the tumour are so inosculated into some of the principal veins and arteries of the natural system, that to remove it by absorption is impossible, and excision would be fatal.

MONTESINOS. Happily, this is but a metaphor; and the body politic, like its crowned head, never dies.

By this time we had reached the bank above Applethwaite. The last question of my companion was one to which I could make no reply, and as he neither talked for triumph, nor I endeavoured to elude the force of his argument, we remained awhile in silence, looking upon the assemblage of dwellings below. Here, and in the adjoining hamlet of Millbeck, the effects of manufactures and of agriculture may be seen and compared. The old cottages are such as the poet and the painter equally delight in beholding. Substantially built of the native stone without mortar, dirtied with no white-lime, and their long low roofs covered with slate, if they had been raised by the magic of some indigenous Amphion's music, the materials could not have adjusted themselves more beautifully in accord with the surrounding scene; and time has still farther harmonized them with weather stains, lichens and moss, short grasses and short fern, and stone plants of various kinds. The ornamented chimnies, round or square, less adorned than those which, like little turrets, crest the houses of the Portugueze peasantry, and yet not less happily suited to their place; the hedge of clipt box beneath the windows, the rose bushes beside the door, the little patch of flower ground with its tall holyocks in front, the garden beside, the bee-hives, and the orchard with its bank of daffodils and snowdrops, (the earliest and the profusest in these parts,) indicate in the owners some portion of ease and leisure, some regard to neatness and comfort, some sense of natural and innocent and healthful enjoyment. The new cottages of the manufacturers, are . . . upon the manufacturing pattern . . . naked, and in a row.

How is it, said I, that every thing which is connected with manufactures, presents such features of unqualified deformity? From the largest of Mammon's temples down to the poorest hovel in which his helotry are stalled, the edifices have all one character. Time cannot mellow them; Nature will neither clothe nor conceal them; and they remain always as offensive to the eye as to the mind!

3 Working Conditions in the Industrial Revolution

The rapid industrialization of Great Britain, added to the hardships of the wars of the French Revolution and Napoleon, created serious conditions among the poor. Many members of the upper classes were troubled by the burgeoning of manufactures and by the use of small children in producing them. The children were a necessary part of the new cotton textile industry for, because of their small size, they could move freely under the machinery to repair broken threads and keep the looms and spindles working. The moral question raised by such employment could not long be ignored, and in 1816 a parliamentary committee was appointed to find out if the employment of children was detrimental to their health and morals.

FROM *Report . . . on the State of the Children Employed . . .*

The first witness is Matthew Baillie, M.D. The Chairman of the Committee is Sir Robert Peel, himself an industrialist and the father of the future Prime Minister.

IN SPEAKING OF THE INJURY to young persons arising from labour, do you mean to speak of labour which requires great bodily exertion?—I did not suppose that children at so early an age were employed in great

Report of the Minutes of Evidence taken before the Select Committee on the State of the Children employed in the Manufactories of the United Kingdom, 25 April—18 June, 1816, pp. 30–1, 46–8, 50–2, 178–81, 222–3.

bodily exertion, but I meant any bodily exertion in which they were confined in a given space, and their minds not allowed to wander into the various channels of thought, and their limbs allowed the sort of irregular exercise which takes place in children who are living in the usual manner.

Is not the state of maturity of children very different in those brought up in the country, to those brought up in town?—With regard to children who are brought up in the country, they are more vigorous; and I have no doubt, in many instances, their progress towards maturity may be more rapid than in children who are reared in a large town.

And your experience has principally been in town?—Entirely, I may say.

Have you been called to give any opinion, or to know the state of health in different manufactories?—I have not.

What is the state of heat, as ascertained by a thermometer, in which children might work without injury?—I should say, that the temperature which is upon the whole most favourable, is about sixty degrees of heat.

In giving your opinion upon this subject, do you take into your consideration the situation in which children would be placed, if, at an early period, they were not employed in such factories?—I do not know that the whole of this pressed on my mind, but certainly it was not absent from it; I drew the comparison between those children as employed in manufactories, and the ordinary employment of children in the country.

Would children of the age of ten be employed in the ordinary business of the country?—No; but they would be doing a good deal of work of various kinds, as going of errands, or weeding, and a thousand employments, which I cannot at present call up to my mind.

That answer seems to refer more particularly to children in the country, as the manufactories are generally in towns, it does not apply to them; therefore the Committee wish to know whether you conceive, if children at an early period of life were prevented by Act of Parliament from working in factories, their situation would be better than it is?—I conceive it would be more favourable to health to be at large, although they might sometimes be not well nourished; and although sometimes they would be in hot rooms, they would have a great deal more time in which they could be playing about, and using their faculties of observation.

Then if those children were left on the parish for support, and many sent to the workhouse, their situation would be better than at present?—I think that children would be better situated in a workhouse, were they not so employed, than in manufactories.

Do you give this as an opinion that you derive from an accurate observation of facts, with respect to the condition of children in factories, or do you give it upon general reasoning?—Upon general reasoning.

Then you are not really acquainted with the condition of children employed in such manufactories?—I am not really acquainted with the condition of children employed in such manufactures; but I mention what I suppose must be more or less the influence of confinement which children are subject to in those manufactories upon their health, from the general principles that guide us in ascertaining the causes that maintain health or lead to sickness, with respect to the human body generally.

In a factory consisting of 875 persons, the annual deaths in which were not more than from two to five, should you conceive that the employment was inconsistent with the health of the people employed?—I should say it does not appear from that statement to have been inconsistent; I conceive, a great many of those children might not be in vigorous health, not in the same health in which they would otherwise be, and yet not be attacked with diseases which would occasion death.

Your answer refers to the number of deaths in a particular year; but if the average for seven years should be about the same, would not you consider that fact as tolerable evidence of the health of the employment?— Indeed I should think so.

Then if in another factory consisting of 289 persons, two only died in the year 1815; and on the 13th of April, one only was sick; would not that afford a tolerable inference of the healthiness of the persons employed in that factory?—It certainly would; but as I stated before, I can easily believe that those children may not be attacked by diseases which should lead to death; but at the same time, be many of them less vigorous than they otherwise would be if employed in the usual manner.

Then in factories, where on the average persons are employed seven years, and where a great portion remain from fourteen to twenty; if the general state of health has been good, would not that be tolerably good evidence of the healthiness of the employment?—I think so.

Have you ever had reason to conceive that there exists in the lower classes of people, a want of affection and tenderness for their children?—I believe you will find very often less affection, both of fathers and mothers for their children in the lower classes, than in the middle ranks: But at the same time there are many strong instances of the purest maternal and paternal affection in the lowest classes of society, where there may be very great difficulty to rear children: they will often submit to every kind of privation respecting themselves, in order to rear the children with some degree of comfort.

Then the lowest class are not the persons where the greatest degree of affection is found for their children?—I think not.

Does not a family press much harder on a poor man, than on any other class?—No doubt.

And is it not of greater importance to him to superintend the care of those children, than to any other class of persons in life?—It must be of more importance to him to superintend, if he can, the education and the bringing up of his children, because in other ranks of life, there are persons who can be procured to do that office for them.

Does not any sickness or want of health in the children of the poor, press upon the parents more than upon any other class of persons?—Certainly.

In the communications you have received from other practitioners, have you ever heard of any great detriment that has occurred to children from too intense employment in manufactories?—I do not recollect that I have ever received a communication upon the subject.

Have you had opportunities of observation upon the condition of the children of the poor not employed in manufactories in large towns?—I have been engaged almost from the beginning of my medical life, in the middle and higher ranks of society.

*   *   *

Sir Gilbert Blane, M.D., was also examined.

May it not happen, by those children being kept employed not in hard labour but in that kind of gentle occupation that gives exercise without superinducing too great fatigue, for twelve hours in a day, in factories, where the air was pure and salutary?—That is a question that, from my want of knowing in detail what is the nature of the employment, I cannot answer; if it was not sedentary but loco-motive, ten hours would not be too much.

Must not a great deal of the power of performance on the part of children, depend on the nourishment and cloathing which they receive?—Not the least doubt much must depend upon the quantity and quality of food.

May not, both in men and animals, an increased degree of maturity be attained in consequence of the food that they receive?—No doubt of it; but there is a greater latitude in the human species than in any other; a man, so speaking, is more an animal of mixed food than any other.

May not children of ten years of age, by being better fed and better care taken of them, be capable of doing more work, without injury to his health, than a child of the same age could have done twenty years ago?—I am clearly of that opinion, from the habits of life, which I have watched with great accuracy.

In referring to the powers of children, are we not to refer, not to what they were, but to what they actually are, from the improvements that have been made?—No doubt of it.

Has it ever occurred to you, to contemplate what has been the increased consumption of animal food within the last fifty years?—I have frequently attended to it, and I think with advantage to mankind, particularly to the young.

Is not the increase of animal food, to young and old, ten times what it was fifty years ago?—It has certainly increased, but I should think that was too high a ratio; it has been increased, to the benefit of all ages, and particularly to the young.

In your observations, has not the consumption of animal food greatly increased within the last fifty years?—It has greatly increased.

Has it not greatly increased within the last twenty years?—Certainly it has, according to my observation.

And that has had a material influence on the strength and health of the people?—I suppose that that has had some share in the decreased mortality which appears.

Is the Committee to understand, that you consider the employment of children, under the age of ten years, to be wholly improper and inconvenient?—By no means wholly improper; I should think if it was limited to five or six hours, that would not only not be pernicious, but salutary.

And you think the employment of children from ten to sixteen, ought not to exceed ten hours a day?—Yes, that might be without prejudice.

You were understood to say, you conceived the state of the atmosphere in which the children worked, was of more importance than the labour itself?—Certainly; they would suffer more from foul air than from the actual labour: the manual labour is the least evil I think.

You say, that the employment of children under ten, might, under certain restrictions, not only be not detrimental, but even beneficial?—I should have no objection to five or six hours.

Are there any restrictions, in point of time or kind of work, that would make it proper to employ children under six years old?—I am so little acquainted with the nature of the occupations in manufactories, I cannot answer that.

Suppose a great number are kept together in the same room, and not exposed to the open air, and in a sedentary posture, or at any rate not taking exercise, do you conceive that at the age of five or six, such occupation, however limited in point of time, is wholesome?—I should apprehend it is wholesome if very limited.

At the age of five or six?—Even as low as that, very limited in time, and in apartments well ventilated and not crowded.

Do you mean, if during the other parts of the day the children should be allowed to play or amuse themselves in the open air?—Most assuredly I understood it so.

Is the proportion between the cubic feet of air in a room, and the number of persons employed in it, of great importance to their health?—Very great; that is a subject I have particularly studied.

In rooms properly ventilated, and where the quantity of respirable air allowed to each person is 1,440 cubic feet, do you think that employment is likely to be prejudicial to such persons?—There is ample space for pure air there; in a hospital there is 700 feet to a patient, and we consider that a safe and proper space, still more so where they are in health and walk about. In a hospital well ventilated, we find 700 cubic feet is a safe and proper space for each patient.

Are you of opinion, that the air in such rooms as have been alluded to, and the employment in them, are likely to be more or less healthy than such rooms as children are employed in by inferior tradesmen, such as tailors and shoemakers?—I apprehend that is a superior degree of ventilation to what they have in the apartments of the labouring poor.

Is it important to the health of children and others, that the temperature of the rooms in which they are employed in winter should be comfortable, and as nearly uniform as is consistent with proper ventilation?—There is no doubt of it; I think comfortable and salutary to be one and the same thing; nature points out what is salutary.

Your attention seems to have been particularly called to the proportion of deaths in different places in this country; do you conceive, that in a factory where in 1811 the number being 873, the deaths in that year being only three; in 1812 the number being 891, the deaths only two; and in 1813 the number being 879, and the deaths only two, such facts to be an indication of the healthiness of the employment in such factory?—It is an indication of the greatest possible health; but it so far exceeds the common course of nature, that if I had it not from such respectable authority I should greatly doubt it.

Would you be surprized at the statement, if you were informed that when children are ill, and likely to die, they are removed from the manufactories?—That alters the case totally.

Are you of opinion, that in another factory, wherein the numbers were 289 employed in 1815, the deaths being two, and where, on the 13th of April only one person out of all that number was sick, such facts are evidence that such factory is healthy?—The same answer; it is evidence of extreme healthiness.

Are you aware, in the most healthy communities, what the proportion of deaths to the persons in life, usually is?—The average in England is one in forty-nine, including Wales one in fifty; and according to the Parliamentary Returns of the beginning of this century, it was one in forty-four; by the Parliamentary Return of 1801.

Healthiness has been somewhat increasing?—Yes.

Did the surprize expressed in a former question, refer to this turning out to be six times less than the average mortality in healthy situations in this country?—To be sure, that made me say it was against the common course of nature; there are no tables that I ever saw, that quoted so high a proportion in the most healthy period of life.

Are you of opinion, that in no situation peculiarly favourable to health in this country, the proportion of deaths is less than that which you have just now stated?—I should have said, had I not been assured of this fact, that that was a rate of mortality that was not to be found any where in the world.

You stated one in forty-four as the average health in healthy districts; the question is, whether, in any particular districts, you have heard of the proportion being smaller than one in forty-four?—Yes; according to the last enumeration the mortality in Cardiganshire is only one in seventy-three, in Monmouthshire one in sixty-four, in Cornwall one in sixty-two, in Gloucestershire one in sixty-one; all the others are under one in sixty. The highest mortality is in the Metropolis and the aguish districts.

Would your surprize of the small mortality cease, if you were informed that no persons are employed under nine years of age, only fifty-nine of the number under ten at the larger factory, and perhaps not forty out of the number above forty years of age, and the factory situated in the healthful county of Ayr, with which you are acquainted?—That renders it somewhat less marvellous.

Have you the means of informing the Committee, what the general mortality is in healthy districts in this country, upon healthy persons between the age of ten and eighteen?—I had lately occasion to make enquiry about that. From some calculations I have made, I found that the mortality in England, between twenty and forty, was about one in eighty.

*   *   *

A deposition was later offered on the part of Charles Pennington, M.D., as a report on the health of the people employed in the mill at Papplewick.

Nottingham, 6th May 1816.

Gentlemen,

Having been desired to communicate to you, as delegates in London from the proprietors of cotton mills and factories in Nottingham and its neighbourhood, my opinion respecting the general state of health of the persons employed in the cotton mills in and near Papplewick, belonging to Mr. James Robinson and Son, I hereby certify to you and to the Honourable the Committee of the House of Commons, that for more than thirty years I have been very frequently called upon in my professional character to attend the family of Mr. Robinson, and the persons employed in his extensive manufactory; and that I have uniformly remarked the most humane attention and careful regard to the health, the morals and the comforts of all engaged in this concern; and that when under medical care, every thing, without any regard to its cost, has been always freely and largely afforded. Further, I may add, that during the greater part of this period, I have had a considerable practice in the town of Nottingham, in a very populous district, for many miles around it, and also in the Infirmary and Lunatic Asylum, amongst all classes and descriptions of people; and after a careful review of the more important circumstances connected with the health of the parties, my conviction is, that the persons employed in the cotton-spinning manufactories are as healthy and strong as any engaged in sedentary pursuits in general; more healthy and strong than the frame-work-knitter; and much more so than the shoemaker and the tailor.

I am, very respectfully, Gentlemen,
Your obedient Servant,
Charles Pennington, M.D.
Honorary Physician to the General Hospital,
Messrs. Stanton and Heygate.   and Physician to the Lunatic Asylum

Mr. Archibald Buchanan, a mill owner, also took the stand.

Do you know of any person whose health was beginning to fail, leaving the manufactory?—I have known many instances of that kind; and I have known many instances of persons of delicate health coming into the manufactory, as being an easy employment.

Did you ever know of a sickly or delicate child coming into the manufactory?—A great many.

And did they, from a more regular life and a more constant supply of food and regular habits, get better?—Their parents had difficulty in getting employment for them otherwise, and they were glad to get them into the works as being easy; there are some parts of it where they may either sit or stand; and there are many parts of the work where lame people can be employed; and gentlemen in the neighbourhood, and frequently parishes, make application to me to have these people taken in to obtain a subsistence.

And from these circumstances, particularly the material one of having a regular supply of good food, did you observe that those children improved in their health?—I have observed very great improvement from their getting good food.

*   *   *

Did you ever, in the course of your visits at the different manufactories, see any establishments . . . under better regulations than those of Messrs. Finlay & Company, and those of Messrs. Phillips & Company?—I suppose there are none better regulated, in general, than that of Messrs. Phillips & Company.

Or than that of Messrs. Finlay & Company?—I have great delicacy in saying that, I believe many others are equally well regulated. I would beg to state to the Committee, that when the girls grow up, we do not object to their going to service; we rather recommend it; they go away for six months, and twelve months; and if they let us know when they wish to return to the works again, we endeavour to employ them. Many of these young women get married, and of course we take no further account of them; after that, we do not enter the deaths of those people.

In the changes that took place in the year 1811, had you reason to think that a considerable proportion of those changes took place in consequence of your dismissing sick persons?—I know no instance of sick persons being dismissed; it must be understood, however, that when these persons become sickly, they go away; and they are received back into the works when they recover, if they are people of good character, and well behaved.

If those persons had quitted the works from sickness, and not quitted the village, would your attention have been directed to them, and would you have considered them as persons employed in the manufactory in your returns?—I certainly should.

Then have you any reason to believe, that on the change, to the extent of twenty persons, supposed to have taken place in 1811, more of those persons were sick, and that a greater proportion of deaths took place among them, than among the persons remaining in the factory?—I do not suppose there was a greater proportion.

Your supposition of course must depend upon the number out of the twenty who remained under your eye in the village?—I understand the twenty all to have gone away.

Do you mean, all to have gone away out of the village?—No; only to have left the works.

Is the account from which you have spoken, prepared by yourself, or by one of the principal persons under your direction?—It was prepared by myself, so far as I could obtain information; it is entered in the hand-writing of one of our clerks.

And has reference to every person employed, during the period you have spoken of, at your works?—At the time that these enquiries were made, and the number of deaths taken, we could have no contemplation of any investigation of this kind; they were taken for the satisfaction of those concerned, and they were taken accurately to the best of my knowledge; at the same time it is possible that a death or two might not be entered.

Have you a conviction of their general accuracy?—I believe it.

Have you any doubt of their accuracy?—I have no reason to doubt it.

Have you reason to suppose, that the years that have been selected were peculiarly healthy, or do you conceive them to be a fair specimen of the state of mortality in the village of Catrine?—The years are not selected, they are the last five years.

Do you suppose that the last four years to which your account refers, were peculiarly healthy, or that they are a fair specimen of the state of mortality in the village of Catrine?—I have no means of knowing the state of mortality in the village; it is a healthy situation, and I can only state that of late years; indeed it has been progressive: the people that we employ are becoming more healthy; that I attribute to a greater degree of cleanliness in the works, but especially to their getting liberal wages, and being well fed and clothed.

*   *   *

Do you know what proportion the persons employed in the manufactory bear to the whole population of the village?—The village contains something above 2,000.

Including those employed in the manufactory?—Yes.

Do you know any thing of the total number of deaths in the village?—I do not.

Do you mean to give to the Committee the impression, that the average number of deaths of the persons employed in the manufactory, at all resembles the total average number of deaths in the village?—I should think that the deaths belonging to the manufactory were less; I have been frequently told by the medical gentleman who attends our people, that in the course of his practice, he finds less disease existing with the people employed in the works, than in the general population of the surrounding country.

Do you mean to lead the Committee to apprehend, that the deaths, upon the remaining eleven hundred who live in the village, are in any thing resembling an equal proportion to that of the deaths in the manufactory?—I am of opinion that they are considerably more; I beg leave to state, that parents with a large family often come to the village and get their children employed; the parents frequently do little or nothing at home, and of course there are a smaller proportion of grown up people in our works than are to be found among the inhabitants of the village.

Those in your works are at the more healthy periods of life?—Yes.

*   *   *

In the population of the village, are the greater proportion of those not now in your works out of employment?—I have stated in my former evidence, that a great number of those who have formerly been employed in the mills have grown up and gone to other trades; a great number of them are masons, joiners, shoemakers, tailors, and in fact, engaged in every kind of trade almost.

And you have not observed, that those people who have been formerly employed in the works, have been affected in their health?—They are very similar to those who have been brought up in the country; and I mentioned also, that tradesmen generally prefer those brought up in the works to people from the country, on account of their having been brought up in industry, and having acquired a great degree of ingenuity.

*   *   *

MR. JOHN MOSS, CALLED IN, AND EXAMINED

Where do you live?—At Preston workhouse.

In Lancashire?—Yes.

What is your occupation?—My present occupation is that of governor of the workhouse.

Were you ever employed as the master of the apprentices at a cotton mill?—I was engaged to attend the apprentice-house at Backbarrow. I was over the children.

*   *   *

Up to what period were they apprenticed?—One-and-twenty.

What were the hours of work?—From five o'clock in the morning till eight at night.

Were fifteen hours in the day the regular hours of work?—Those were their regular hours of work.

Was that the regular time all the year through?—Yes.

What time was allowed for meals?—Half an hour for breakfast and half an hour for dinner.

*   *   *

Had they any refreshment in the afternoon?—Yes, they had their drinking taken to the mill; their bagging, they call it.

You mean luncheon?—Yes.

Did they work while they ate their afternoon refreshment?—Yes.

They had no cessation after dinner till eight o'clock at night?—No.

At what hour was the breakfast?—At seven in the morning; they came to their breakfast at seven o'clock, and then the bell rang for them at half past seven.

Did they leave the mill at breakfast time?—Yes, they always left the mill and came to the house.

What was the dinner hour?—Twelve o'clock.

And at what time did they return to the mill?—Half past twelve.

Did they, beyond working those fifteen hours, make up for any loss of time?—Yes, always.

Did the children actually work fourteen hours in the day?—Yes.

And one hour was allowed for the two meals, making fifteen hours in the whole?—Yes.

When the works were stopped for the repair of the mill, or for any want of cotton, did the children afterwards make up for the loss of that time?—Yes.

When making up lost time, how long did they continue working at night?— Till nine o'clock, and sometimes later; sometimes ten.

Was this before the Apprentice Bill or after?—It was last year, and it is in practice now.

How long were they making up lost time?—I have known them to be three weeks or more making up lost time.

Have you known them for three weeks together working from five in the morning till nine or ten at night, with the exception of the hour for meals?—Yes, I have.

What time did they rise from bed?—I always got up at half past four to get them ready to be at the mill by five.

How far was their sleeping room from the mill?—It might be not above a hundred yards; hardly so much.

Did they rise at half past four in the winter season?—They were always to be at the mill by five o'clock winter and summer, and never later.

Were there two mills?—Yes.

When you had only water for one mill, did the children work night and day?—When there was only water for one mill, one worked in the day and the other at night.

Have you ever known the children work all night on Saturday, until six o'clock on Sunday morning?—Yes, I have once; they have gone to work at eight o'clock on Saturday night, and stayed till six on Sunday morning.

At what hour on Sunday night did those children begin to work again? —They have begun at twelve o'clock on Sunday night again, and worked till five in the morning; then the other children for the day began at the other mill, and worked till eight at night.

Did they work as late on Saturday night as on other nights?—Always the same; I never knew any abatement.

Did any children work on the Sundays as cleaners of the machinery?— Yes.

Did they do this regularly?—Regularly every Sunday; I do not know that ever they missed one Sunday while I was there.

Through the year?—Yes.

How many hours did they work on a Sunday?—Their orders were from six till twelve.

Did you remonstrate against this?—Yes, I did.

Frequently?—Yes.

What was the consequence of your remonstrance?—It was never much better; there were not so many went to the mill; I believe that they went from their own accord sometimes, and I wished the book-keeper to give in a paper of the names of those who were to attend.

Did the children take it in rotation?—It was just according to what wanted cleaning.

Who gave orders what children were to work on a Sunday?—The book-keeper sent me a written note of the names of those who were to attend.

Did he give you a written order in consequence of your remonstrance? —Yes.

Do you remember any Sunday when they did not work while you were at the mills?—I do not remember one Sunday when they did not go to work.

If they had left off work a little earlier on Saturday, could not they have avoided the necessity of going to the mills on a Sunday?—Yes.

Were the children paid for the Sunday-work?—Yes.

Did the children ever attend church?—Yes.

Would the children rather get money by working on a Sunday than attend church?—I thought there was a motive, which made me put a stop to it, by having a written order who was to attend.

Did they absent themselves sometimes from church, under the pretence of going to the mill to clean the machinery?—Yes.

Did the overlookers ever give you any orders for the children to work till twelve o'clock on Saturday night?—Yes.

Did you remonstrate against this also?—Yes.

For what reason?—Because we had the children to wash and clean after they had done work on Saturday night, therefore it was late before we got to bed; but they have sometimes worked till ten, the whole of the children; and when they have been short of water, that set that went on to work at eight at night was worked till twelve.

Did the masters ever express any concern for such excessive labour?—No.

Was it at the desire of the proprietors of the mill, or of the overlookers, that the children worked till twelve o'clock on Saturday night?—It was the master of the mill that wished them to work till twelve o'clock at night, when they were short of water; but it was the overlookers that wished the whole of them to work till twelve o'clock at night, in order to make up lost time, that they might get done the sooner; the whole of them never did work together later than ten.

Were they very strict in keeping them to their time?—Yes.

Did the children sit or stand to work?—Stand.

The whole of their time?—Yes.

Were there any seats in the mill?—None.

Were they usually much fatigued at night?—Yes, some of them were very much fatigued.

Where did they sleep?—They slept in the apprentice-house.

Did you inspect their beds?—Yes, every night.

For what purpose?—Because there were always some of them missing, some sometimes might be run away, others sometimes I have found have been asleep in the mill.

Upon the mill-floor?—Yes.

Did the children frequently lie down upon the mill-floor at night when their work was over, and fall asleep before their supper?—I have found them frequently upon the mill-floors, after the time they should have been in bed.

At what time did they go to bed?—Nine o'clock was their hour, when they worked their usual time.

In summer time did you allow them to sit up a little later?—Yes, sometimes till half past nine.

Were any children injured by the machinery?—Very frequently.

Were their fingers often crushed?—Very often their fingers were caught; and one had his arm broken.

Were any of the children deformed?—Yes, several of them were deformed; there were two or three that were very crooked.

Do you know whether those children were straight when they first came to the mill?—They told me they were.

Who told you they were?—The children themselves.

Were any of the children in-kneed, or what is called knock-kneed?— Yes, there were ten or a dozen of them, I dare say, that were in-kneed.

Did you understand from them whether they were so when they came to the mill?—I do not know that they were.

Do you think they were not?—I am pretty sure some of them were not, but some of them were lame when they came.

Did the parish officers of the parishes to which they belonged, ever come to the mills to visit and inspect the children?—No; there was one from Liverpool; the overseer of Liverpool.

Do you remember his name?—Hardman, I believe.

Was there any other inspection by magistrates, or any other persons?— No, there was no magistrates ever came into the childrens house.

Is the mill in a healthy situation?—Very.

Remarkably so?—Yes.

As the children grew up, did they in general appear to be healthy, or otherwise?—There were some who were very healthy children, and there were others that were sickly looking.

What was their general appearance?—Their general appearance was as well as most of the farmers children, some of them; some of them looked sickly, but then they were not sick.

They appeared to be sick, but were not so?—Yes; we scarcely ever had any sickness in the house.

How many died during the year you were at the mill?—There was only one.

How were the children lodged?—They had very good lodgings when we left them.

Had they good lodgings when you first went there?—No.

Did you make any complaints of their bedding when you first went?— Yes.

Will you state to the Committee what was the condition of their bedding when you first went?—When I first went there; their bedding was very bad, they had only a blanket to lie on, and a thin blanket to lie at top, and a horse cover, and some of them were very bad.

Could they be preserved cleanly with sleeping only on blankets?—They were not altogether clean.

Did you make complaint of that?—Yes.

Did the parish officer from Liverpool complain of it?—Yes.

Was it in consequence of his complaints and yours, that the bedding was improved?—Yes, it was; we got after that sheets and covers for every bed, and there never were sheets for any bed in the house I believe, before.

Did they spin fine or coarse yarn at those mills?—Very coarse.

Were the rooms as warm as where they spin fine?—No, I believe not.

Do you understand that they require greater heat for fine threads?—I have heard them say so; they have no heat in their rooms in the summer, in the winter they have heat from steam.

Were the children fed well?—Very well.

Before your time at Backbarrow mill, were the children turned out on the high road to beg their way to their former parishes, when the former proprietor stopped payment?—I was informed they were.

Did you converse with any of the children that were so turned out?—Yes.

Were they taken from the mill in a cart, and then turned adrift near the sands on the Lancaster road?—Yes, I was informed they were.

Do you know what became of them afterwards?—There was one of them I heard was taken in at Caton factory, and employed there for some time; and I heard there were some of them taken into Lancaster workhouse.

Did you hear that the gentlemen of Lancaster complained of this inhumanity?—Yes.

Were any fetched back in consequence of these complaints?—Yes, I believe there were.

Were they then turned over to Messrs. Ainsworth the present proprietors?—Yes.

After they had served out their apprenticeship to Messrs. Ainsworth, were they not compelled to serve extra time, under the pretence that so much time was lost by being turned out on the road and obliged to go to Lancaster?—Yes, there was one boy out of his time while I was there, and when the day came his master said that he had to serve six weeks, I think, longer, in consequence of his having run away; he said he never had ran away, he was turned out, and he had worked at Caton factory, and they made him serve that time out; his name is Henry Carter.

Do you know of Messrs. Watson's apprentices being turned out in the same manner?—I have heard it said so, but I never knew anything of it.

Were the children bad in their morals?—Yes, they were.

How did they behave one to another?—They did not behave well one to another.

Who looked over them in the mill?—Generally the older apprentices were overlookers over the younger ones.

Did the bigger boys beat the others?—Yes.

Frequently?—Yes.

What was the general character of the children?—Very bad characters.

What was the reason you left the mill?—It was in consequence of their bad behaviour.

4 Evaluation of the Industrial Revolution

Thomas Babington Macaulay (1800–1859) is most generally remembered for his history of England in the seventeenth century. He was also an essayist of devastating wit and power. Nothing was more calculated to arouse his ire than an attack on the idea of progress; and Southey's romanticism seemed to him such an attack. This review reveals Macaulay at his polemical best.

FROM Southey's Colloquies BY T. B. MACAULAY

IT WOULD BE SCARCELY POSSIBLE for a man of Mr. Southey's talents and acquirements to write two volumes so large as those before us, which should be wholly destitute of information and amusement. Yet we do not remember to have read with so little satisfaction any equal quantity of matter, written by any man of real abilities. We have, for some time past, observed with great regret the strange infatuation which leads the Poet Laureate to abandon those departments of literature in which he might excel, and to lecture the public on sciences of which he has still the very alphabet to learn. He has now, we think, done his worst. The subject which he has at last undertaken to treat is one which demands all the highest intellectual and moral qualities of a philosophical statesman, an understanding at once comprehensive and acute, a heart at once upright and charitable. Mr. Southey brings to the task two faculties which were never, we believe, vouchsafed in measure so copious to any human being, the faculty of believing without a reason, and the faculty of hating without a provocation.

It is, indeed, most extraordinary, that a mind like Mr. Southey's, a mind richly endowed in many respects by nature, and highly cultivated by study, a mind which has exercised considerable influence on the most enlightened generation of the most enlightened people that ever existed, should be utterly destitute of the power of discerning truth from falsehood. Yet such is the

Critical and Historical Essays contributed to the Edinburgh Review by Lord Macaulay, I (1903), 205, 207, 215–8.

fact. Government is to Mr. Southey one of the fine arts. He judges of a theory, of a public measure, of a religion or a political party, of a peace or a war, as men judge of a picture or a statue, by the effect produced on his imagination. A chain of associations is to him what a chain of reasoning is to other men; and what he calls his opinions are in fact merely his tastes.

*   *   *

Now in the mind of Mr. Southey reason has no place at all, as either leader or follower, as either sovereign or slave. He does not seem to know what an argument is. He never uses arguments himself. He never troubles himself to answer the arguments of his opponents. It has never occurred to him, that a man ought to be able to give some better account of the way in which he has arrived at his opinions than merely that it is his will and pleasure to hold them. It has never occurred to him that there is a difference between assertion and demonstration, that a rumour does not always prove a fact, that a single fact, when proved, is hardly foundation enough for a theory, that two contradictory propositions cannot be undeniable truths, that to beg the question is not the way to settle it, or that when an objection is raised, it ought to be met with something more convincing than "scoundrel" and "blockhead."

*   *   *

We now come to the conversations which pass between Mr. Southey and Sir Thomas More, or rather between two Southeys, equally eloquent, equally angry, equally unreasonable, and equally given to talking about what they do not understand. Perhaps we could not select a better instance of the spirit which pervades the whole book than the passages in which Mr. Southey gives his opinion of the manufacturing system. There is nothing which he hates so bitterly. It is, according to him, a system more tyrannical than that of the feudal ages, a system of actual servitude, a system which destroys the bodies and degrades the minds of those who are engaged in it. He expresses a hope that the competition of other nations may drive us out of the field; that our foreign trade may decline; and that we may thus enjoy a restoration of national sanity and strength. But he seems to think that the extermination of the whole manufacturing population would be a blessing, if the evil could be removed in no other way.

Mr. Southey does not bring forward a single fact in support of these views; and, as it seems to us, there are facts which lead to a very different conclusion. In the first place, the poor-rate is very decidedly lower in the manufacturing than in the agricultural districts. If Mr. Southey will look over the Parliamentary returns on this subject, he will find that the amount of parochial relief required by the labourers in the different counties of England is almost exactly in inverse proportion to the degree in which the manufacturing system has been introduced into those counties. The returns for the years ending in March 1825, and in March 1828, are now before us. In the former year we find the poor-rate highest in Sussex, about twenty shillings to every inhabitant. Then come Buckinghamshire, Essex, Suffolk, Bedfordshire, Huntingdonshire, Kent, and Norfolk. In all these the rate is above fifteen shillings a head. We will not go through the whole. Even in Westmoreland and the North Riding of Yorkshire, the rate is at more than eight shillings. In Cumberland and Monmouthshire, the most fortunate of all the agricultural districts, it is at six shillings. But in the West Riding of Yorkshire, it is as low as five shillings; and when we come to Lancashire, we find it at four shillings, one fifth of what it is in Sussex. The returns of the year ending in March 1828 are a little, and but a little, more un-favourable to the manufacturing districts. Lancashire, even in that season of distress, required a smaller poor-rate than any other district, and little more than one fourth of the poor-rate raised in Sussex. Cumberland alone, of the agricultural districts, was as well off as the West Riding of Yorkshire. These facts seem to indicate that the manufacturer is both in a more comfortable and in a less dependent situation than the agricultural labourer.

As to the effect of the manufacturing system on the bodily health, we must beg leave to estimate it by a standard far too low and vulgar for a mind so imaginative as that of Mr. Southey, the proportion of births and deaths. We know that, during the growth of this atrocious system, this new misery, to use the phrases of Mr. Southey, this new enormity, this birth of a portentous age, this pest which no man can approve whose heart is not seared or whose understanding has not been darkened, there has been a great diminution of mortality, and that this diminution has been greater in the manufacturing towns than any where else. The mortality still is, as it always was, greater in towns than in the country. But the difference has diminished in an extraordinary degree. There is the best reason to believe that the annual mortality of Manchester, about the middle of the last century, was one in twenty-eight. It is now reckoned at one in forty-five. In Glasgow and Leeds a similar improvement has taken place. Nay, the rate of mortality in those three great capitals of the manufacturing districts is now considerably less than it was, fifty years ago, over England and Wales, taken together, open country and all. We might with some plausibility maintain that the people live longer because they are better fed, better lodged, better clothed, and better attended in sickness, and that these improvements are owing to that increase of national wealth which the manufacturing system has produced.

Much more might be said on this subject. But to what end? It is not from bills of mortality and statistical tables that Mr. Southey has learned his political creed. He cannot stoop to study the history of the system which he abuses, to strike the balance between the good and evil which it has pro-duced, to compare district with district, or generation with generation. We will give his own reason for his opinion, the only reason which he gives for it, in his own words:—

"We remained awhile in silence looking upon the assemblage of dwellings below. Here, and in the adjoining hamlet of Millbeck, the effects of manufactures and of agriculture may be seen and compared. The old cottages are such as the poet and the painter equally delight in beholding. Substantially built of the native stone without mortar, dirtied with no white lime, and their long low roofs covered with slate, if they had been raised by the magic of some indigenous Amphion's music, the materials could not have adjusted themselves more beautifully in accord with the surrounding scene; and time has still further harmonized them with weather stains, lichens, and moss, short grasses, and short fern, and stone-plants of various kinds. The ornamented chimneys, round or square, less adorned than those which, like little turrets, crest the houses of the Portuguese peasantry; and yet not less happily suited to their place, the hedge of clipt box beneath the windows, the rose-bushes beside the door, the little patch of flower ground, with its tall hollyhocks in front; the garden beside, the beehives, and the orchard with its bank of daffodils and snow-drops, the earliest and the profusest in these parts, indicate in the owners some portion of ease and leisure, some regard to neatness and comfort, some sense of natural, and innocent, and healthful enjoyment. The new cottages of the manufacturers are upon the manufacturing pattern—naked, and in a row.

"How is it," said I, "that every thing which is connected with manufactures presents such features of unqualified deformity? From the largest of Mammon's temples down to the poorest hovel in which his helotry are stalled, these edifices have all one character. Time will not mellow them; nature will neither clothe nor conceal them; and they will remain always as offensive to the eye as to the mind."

Here is wisdom. Here are the principles on which nations are to be governed. Rose-bushes and poor-rates, rather than steam-engines and independence. Mortality and cottages with weather-stains, rather than health and long life with edifices which time cannot mellow. We are told, that our age has invented atrocities beyond the imagination of our fathers; that society has been brought into a state compared with which extermination would be a blessing; and all because the dwellings of cotton-spinners are naked and rectangular. Mr. Southey has found out a way, he tells us, in which the effects of manufactures and agriculture may be compared. And what is this way? To stand on a hill, to look at a cottage and a factory, and to see which is the prettier. Does Mr. Southey think that the body of the English peasantry live, or ever lived, in substantial or ornamented cottages, with box-hedges, flower-gardens, beehives, and orchards? If not, what is his parallel worth? We despise those mock philosophers, who think that they serve the cause of science by depreciating literature and the fine arts. But if any thing could excuse their narrowness of mind, it would be such a book as this. It is not strange that, when one enthusiast makes the picturesque the test of political good, another should feel inclined to proscribe altogether the pleasures of taste and imagination.

> *The work from which this selection is taken has long been regarded as the standard work in its field. First published in 1906, it utilized the full panoply of the historian's art and resources to reach an essentially negative judgment on the immediate effect of the Industrial Revolution on the working men who were caught up in it.*

FROM The Industrial Revolution in the Eighteenth Century BY PAUL MANTOUX

INTERMIXED WITH THE MEN'S GRIEVANCES against machinery was their hatred of the factory. The feeling of repulsion which it aroused is easily understood, as, to a man used to working at home, or in a small workshop, factory discipline was intolerable. Even though at home he had to work long hours to make up for the lowness of his wage, yet he could begin and stop at will, and without regular hours. He could divide up the work as he chose, come and go, rest for a moment, and even, if he chose, be idle for days together. Even if he worked in the master-manufacturer's house, his freedom, though less complete, was still fairly great. He did not feel that there was an impassable gulf between himself and his employer, and their relations still retained something of a personal character. He was not bound by hard and fast regulations, as relentless and as devoid of sympathy as the machinery itself. He saw little difference between going to a factory and entering a barracks or a prison. This is why the first generation of manufacturers often found real difficulty in obtaining labour. They would have found it still more difficult, had there not been a floating population available, which the changes in rural conditions were driving from agriculture into industry and from the country to the towns. Other workers were attracted from the poorer parts of the Kingdom, from the bogs of Ireland and from the mountains of Scotland or Wales. Thus the origin of factory labour is to be found partly in a class of men forcibly uprooted from their employment, and partly among populations to whom industry offered better opportunities than did their former employment.

From *The Industrial Revolution in the Eighteenth Century,* rev. ed. (1928), pp. 419–28, 486–9, by Paul Mantoux, translated by Marjorie Vernon. Reprinted by permission of Harcourt, Brace & World, Inc., Mrs. Mathilde Mantoux, and Jonathan Cape Ltd., London.

In the textile trades the manufacturers found another way out of the difficulty, by resorting largely to women and child labour. Spinning was quickly learned and needed little strength, while for certain processes the small size of the children and their delicacy of touch made them the best aids to the machines. They were preferred, too, for other and more conclusive reasons. Their weakness made them docile, and they were more easily reduced to a state of passive obedience than grown men. They were also very cheap. Sometimes they were given a trifling wage, which varied between a third and a sixth of an adult wage; and sometimes their only payment was food and lodging. Lastly they were bound to the factory by indentures of apprenticeship, for at least seven years, and usually until they were twenty-one. It was obviously to the spinners' interest to employ as many as possible and thus to reduce the number of workmen. The first Lancashire factories were full of children. Sir Robert Peel had over a thousand in his workshops at once.

The majority of these wretched children were paupers, supplied (one might almost say sold) by the parishes where they belonged. Especially during the first period of machine industry, when factories were built outside, and often far from, the towns, manufacturers would have found it impossible to recruit the labour they needed from the immediate neighbourhood. And the parishes on their side were only too anxious to get rid of their paupers. Regular bargains, beneficial to both parties, if not to the children, who were dealt with as mere merchandise, were entered into between the spinners on the one hand and the Poor Law authorities on the other. Lots of fifty, eighty or a hundred children were supplied and sent like cattle to the factory, where they remained imprisoned for many years. Certain parishes drove even better bargains and stipulated that the buyer should take idiots in the proportion of one to every twenty children sent. At the beginning, these "parish apprentices" were the only children employed in the factories. The workmen, very justifiably, refused to send their own. But unfortunately this resistance did not last long, as they were soon driven by want to a step which at first had so much horrified them.

The only extenuating circumstance in the painful events which we have now to recount as shortly as we can, was that forced child labour was no new evil. In the domestic system of manufacture, children were exploited as a matter of course. Among the Birmingham ironmongers, apprenticeship began at seven years of age. Among the weavers of the North and the South-west, children worked at five or even four years old, as soon in fact as they were considered capable of attention and obedience. Far from regarding this with indignation, men at that time thought it an admirable system. Yarranton recommended the establishment of "industrial schools" such as he had seen in Germany. There, two hundred little girls, under a matron's rod, sat spinning without a moment's relaxation and in complete silence, and were beaten if they did not spin quickly or well enough: "In these parts I speak of, a man that has most children lives best; whereas here he that has most is poorest. There the children enrich the father, but here beggar him." When Defoe visited Halifax, he was lost in admiration at the sight of four-year-old children earning their living like grown-up people. William Pitt's statement on child labour, which Michelet, with his usual exaggeration of sentiment and language, quoted against him as though it were a crime, was only a common-place reference to an accepted opinion.

It might be said that in the earlier forms of industry the child was at any rate an apprentice in the true sense, for he learned a trade, instead of merely being a part of the plant, as he was in the factory. But real apprenticeship could only begin when the child was old enough to benefit by it, and therefore for several years the child could only be a workman's drudge, paid either nothing or next to nothing. It might also be said that the conditions under which the child lived were less unfavourable to its physical development; but, with regard to hygiene, we know only too well the condition of the domestic workshop. Was it kindly treated and not overworked? Under the sting of necessity, parents were often the most exacting, if not the harshest of taskmasters.

But, even with these reservations, we must acknowledge that the fate of these parish apprentices, in the early spinning mills, was particularly miserable. Completely at the mercy of their employers, kept in isolated buildings, far from anyone who might take pity on their sufferings, they endured a cruel servitude. Their working day was limited only by their complete exhaustion, and lasted fourteen, sixteen and even eighteen hours. The foreman, whose wages were dependent on the amount of work done in each workshop, did not permit them to relax their efforts for a minute. In most factories forty minutes were allowed for the chief or the only meal of the day, and of these about twenty were taken up in cleaning the machines. In some factories work went on ceaselessly day and night, so that the machines might never stop. In such cases, the children were divided up into shifts, and "the beds never got cold." Accidents were very common, especially towards the end of the over-long day, when the exhausted children almost fell asleep at their work. The tale never ended of fingers cut off and limbs crushed in the wheels.

Discipline was savage, if the word discipline can be applied to such indescribable brutality, and sometimes such refined cruelty, as was exercised at will on defenceless creatures. The well-known catalogue of the sufferings of the factory apprentice, Robert Blincoe, makes one sick with horror. At Lowdham (near Nottingham), whither he was sent in 1799 with a batch of about eighty other boys and girls, they were only whipped. It is true that the whip was in use from morning till night, not only as a punishment for the slightest fault, but also to stimulate industry and to keep them awake when they were dropping with weariness. But at the factory at Litton matters were very different. There, the employer, one Ellice Needham, hit the children with his fists and with a riding whip, he kicked them, and one of his little attentions was to pinch their ears until his nails met through the flesh. The foremen were even worse, and one of them, Robert Woodward, used to devise the most ingenious tortures. It was he who was responsible for such inventions as hanging Blincoe up by his wrists over a machine at work, so that he was obliged to keep his knees bent up, making him work almost naked in winter, with heavy weights on his shoulders, and filing down his teeth. The wretched child had been so knocked about that his scalp was one sore all over. By way of curing him, his hair was torn out by means of a cap of pitch. If the victims of these horrors tried to escape, their feet were put in irons. Many tried to commit suicide, and one girl, who took advantage of a moment when the supervision relaxed and threw herself into the river, thus regained her freedom: she was sent away, as her employer "was afraid the example might be contagious."

Of course, not all factories witnessed such scenes, but they were less rare than their incredible horror would lead one to suppose, and were repeated until a system of strict control was set up. Even if they had not been ill-treated, excessive labour, lack of sleep and the nature of the work forced on children during the critical period of their growth, would have been quite enough to ruin their health and deform their bodies. The food, too, was often bad and insufficient. They had black bread, oatmeal porridge and rancid bacon. At Litton Mill the apprentices used to struggle with the pigs fattening in the yard, in order to get some of the food in their troughs. The factories were usually unhealthy, as their builders cared as little for health as they did for beauty. The ceilings were low in order to economize as much space as possible, the windows were narrow and almost always closed. In the cotton mills, fluff filled the air and gave rise to serious lung diseases. In flax-spinning mills, where wet spinning was usual, the air was saturated with moisture and the workers' clothes were dripping wet. Overcrowding in unventilated rooms, where the atmosphere was further vitiated by candle smoke at night, favoured the spreading of a contagious disorder resembling prison fever. The first cases of this "factory fever" broke out near Manchester in 1784. It very soon spread to nearly all the industrial districts and there were many deaths. Lastly, the promiscuity of both workshops and dormitories gave scope for immorality, and this was, unfortunately, encouraged by the bad behaviour of some of the employers and foremen, who took advantage of it to satisfy their low instincts. Thus to a puritan conscience, the factory, with its mixture of depravity and suffering, of barbarity and vice, offered a perfect picture of hell.

Among those who lived through the cruel period of apprenticeship, many bore its brand for life in the shape of crooked backs, and limbs deformed by rickets or mutilated by accidents with machinery. With "flaccid features, a stunted growth, very often tumid bellies they were already marked down as the victims of all the infections to which, during their later life, they were but too frequently exposed. Their moral and intellectual condition was no better. They left the factory ignorant and corrupt. During their miserable period of servitude not only did they receive no teaching of any kind, but in spite of the formal clauses of their indenture of apprenticeship, they did not even acquire enough technical knowledge to enable them to earn their living. They had learned nothing beyond the mechanical routine to which they had been bound during so many long hard years, and they were thus condemned to remain mere slaves, tied to the factory as of old the serf to the soil.

It must not be assumed that the status of all workers under the factory system was like that of the apprentices in the spinning mills. But, even though adults were not treated with quite the same revolting cruelty, their life in the factory was hard enough. They, too, suffered from too many working hours, from overcrowded and unhealthy workshops, and from tyrannical foremen and overseers. With them, the despotic employer, instead of physical violence, resorted to fraud; one of the most frequent abuses of which the workmen had to complain was that, in order to lengthen the working day, of which every minute meant money to the employer, they were literally robbed of their rest hours. During the dinner hour, the speed of the factory clock appeared miraculously to accelerate, so that work was resumed five or ten minutes before the hour had actually struck. Sometimes the means used to the same end were even simpler and less hypocritical: the meal times and closing times were at the discretion of the employer, and the workers were forbidden to carry watches.

Here we come to the real cause of the evils attributed to machine industry, namely the absolute and uncontrolled power of the capitalist. In this, the heroic age of great undertakings, it was acknowledged, admitted and even proclaimed with brutal candour. It was the employer's own business, he did as he chose, and did not consider that any other justification of his conduct was necessary. He owed his employees wages, and, once those were paid, the men had no further claim on him: put shortly, this was the attitude of the employer as to his rights and his duties. A cotton spinner, on being asked whether he did anything to help sick apprentices, answered: "When we engage a child, it is with the approbation of the parents, and it is an engagement to give a certain quantity of money for a certain quantity of labour. If the labour is not performed, the child is supported by the parents. —Then there is no security afforded to the child, that in sickness the master will support it?—It is an act of bounty in the master." Pure bounty, indeed, on which it was wiser not to count. The same man, when questioned as to why he had decided to stop his machinery at night, explained that he did it in order to allow water to accumulate in a tank, as the stream of the neighbouring river was insufficient: "Then if the stream had been more ample, you would have continued your night work?—As long as the trade had been sufficiently lucrative.—Then there is nothing now to restrain you from working day and night, but want of water or want of trade?—I know of no law to restrain me for so doing: I never heard of any." This was unanswerable, so long as the law remained unchanged.

*   *   *

In the first decade of the nineteenth century, which closes the period we set out to study, the industrial revolution was far from being completed. The use of machinery was still limited to certain industries, and in these industries to certain specialities or certain districts. Side by side with great metal works such as Soho and Coalbrookdale the small workshops of the Birmingham toyman and of the Sheffield cutlers continued to exist, and survived for many decades. Side by side with the Lancashire cotton mills and the West Riding woollen mills, thousands of weavers went on working at home on their old hand looms. Steam, which was to multiply and generalize the results of all other mechanical inventions, had hardly begun its triumphant progress. Nevertheless the modern industrial system did already exist, with all its essential features, and it is possible to detect, in the developments which had taken place at that time, the main characteristics of the great change.

From the technical point of view the industrial revolution consists in the invention and use of processes which make it possible to speed up and constantly to increase production: some are mechanical processes, as in the textile industries, others chemical, as in the metal-working industries; they help either to prepare the raw material, or to determine the form of the finished product, and the phrase machine industry is inadequate to the variety and to the possibilities offered by such developments. The invention of such processes (at least in the beginning) owed little to conclusions drawn from purely scientific discoveries. It is an established fact that most of the first inventors were anything but scientists. They were technical men who, being faced with a practical problem, used their natural faculties and their expert knowledge of the habits and needs of the industry to solve it. Highs, Crompton, Hargreaves, Dudley, Darby and Cort were men of this type. A few others, such as Wyat and Cartwright, undertook their researches instinctively and out of pure curiosity, without either scientific or professional training. Under the pressure of necessity, and on purely concrete data, they set to work without a definite plan, and only reached their goal after much groping in the dark. They represent economic necessity, silently and powerfully moulding men to its will, overcoming obstacles and forging its own instruments. Science came later, and brought its immense reserves of power to bear on the development which had already begun, thus giving at once to partial developments in different industries a common direction and a common speed. This is specially noticeable in the case of Watt and the steam engine. Thus two streams from different sources met, and though it was to their combined power that the industrial revolution owed its actual size and strength, yet the change had already begun and its first results were conspicuous.

From the economic point of view, the industrial revolution is characterized by the concentration of capital and the growth of large undertakings, the existence and working of which, from being only exceptional, came to be the normal conditions of industry. Though, not without reason, this concentration is often considered as the result of technical inventions, yet to a certain extent it preceded such inventions. It was essentially a commercial phenomenon, and was connected with the gradual hold obtained by merchants over industry. Not only was it accompanied, but it was also prepared, by the expansion of trade and credit. Its necessary conditions were internal security, the development of communications and of maritime trade. The historical transition between the master craftsman of the middle ages and the modern industrialist was provided by the merchant manufacturer. We find him at first, so to speak, on the margin of industry, with the sole function of linking up producers with markets which were becoming too large and too distant for them. Later on, as his capital grew and the manufacturer came to rely on him more and more, he became the master of production, and finally the owner of all raw material, buildings and equipment, while independent workmen were degraded to the rank of mere wage-earners. This concentration of the means of production in the hands of capitalists who were more concerned with trade than with industry is a fact of paramount importance. No doubt "manufacture," with the great number of men it employed, the highly specialized division of its labour, and its many likenesses to the factory system, was a more striking fact, but it played a much smaller part in the evolution of industry. It marked a stage on the road, but a stage no sooner reached than passed. Economists, studying this evolution, have conceived and described it as a simple development, one phase following another like the different parts of a geometrical curve. But to the eyes of the historian a movement of such complexity is more like a river, which does not always flow at the same pace, but sometimes slackens its course, sometimes rushes on, now running through narrow gorges and now spreading out over the plain, now breaking up into many divergent branches, and now winding about, so that it seems to curve back on itself. Merely to enumerate the different points it passes by, is not to describe it. To do this, we must follow, step by step, its varied winding course, which in spite of its changes of direction, remains continuous like the slope which bears it to its end.

From the social point of view, the industrial revolution had such extensive and profound results that it would be presumptuous for us to attempt to summarize them in a short formula. Even though, unlike political revolutions, it did not actually alter the legal form of society, yet it modified its very substance. It gave birth to social classes whose progress and mutual opposition fill the history of our times. It would be easy, by quoting some of the facts mentioned in this very book, to try and show that, in this respect, there has been no revolution, that the same social classes were already in existence, that their opposition had begun long before, its nature and cause always remaining the same. One of the objects we have always kept in mind was precisely to show the continuity of the historical process underlying even the most rapid changes. None of these changes took place suddenly, as by a miracle, but each of them had been expected, prepared and outlined before it actually took place. It would be an equal error either to undervalue those preliminaries, or to take them for what they only foreshadowed. We know that there were machines before the era of machinery, "manufacture" before factories, combinations and strikes before the formation of industrial capitalism and of the "factory proletariat." But, in the slow-moving mass of society, a new element does not make itself felt immediately. And we have not only to note its presence, but its relation to its environment and, as it were, the space it occupies, in history. The industrial revolution is precisely the expansion of undeveloped forces, the sudden growth and blossoming of seeds which had for many years lain hidden or asleep.

After the beginning of the nineteenth century the growth of the factory system was visible to all. It was already influencing the distribution, as well as the material condition, of the population. To the factory system were due the importance and sudden prosperity of districts such as Lancashire, South Wales and part of the Lowlands of Scotland, which, until then, had been considered as being among the least prosperous parts of the country. It was the factory system which, following on the redistribution of landed property, quickened the migration of the rural population towards the factories. When the census of 1811 was taken, sixty or seventy per cent. of the inhabitants in the counties of Middlesex, Warwickshire, Yorkshire and Lancashire were employed in trade or industry, and at least fifty per cent. of those of Cheshire, Leicestershire, Nottinghamshire and Staffordshire. In these new centres, full of such intense activity, with their contrasting extremes of wealth and poverty, the data of the social problem, much as we know them to-day, could already be descried. The moment was not far off when that problem was to be defined for the first time by Robert Owen, in his *Letter to the Manufacturers of England* and his *Observations on the Consequences of the Factory System*. And he spoke not for England alone, but for all the nations of the West, for while the factory system continued to develop in the country of its birth, it had already begun to spread to other countries. It had made its appearance on the Continent, and from that time onward its history was no longer English but European—until it extended to the whole world.

*The Hammonds, both educated at Oxford, could find little
good in the Industrial Revolution. To them, it was compa-
rable to slavery, and they make their case with skill and
verve.*

FROM *The Rise of Modern Industry*

BY JOHN L. AND BARBARA HAMMOND

ROME IMPORTED SLAVES to work in Italy: Englishmen counted it one
of the advantages of the slave trade that it discouraged the competition of
British colonists with British manufacturers. For the slaves were chiefly
needed for industries like sugar planting, in which Englishmen at home were
not engaged. Thus it might be argued that England had escaped the fate of
Rome and that she so used the slave trade as to make it a stimulus rather
than a discouragement to native energy and skill.

Yet England did not escape the penalty. For it was under this shadow
that the new industrial system took form and grew, and the immense power
with which invention had armed mankind was exercised at first under
conditions that reproduced the degradation of the slave trade. The factory
system was not like war or revolution a deliberate attack on society: it was
the effort of men to use will, energy, organization and intelligence for the
service of man's needs. But in adapting this new power to the satisfaction of
its wants England could not escape from the moral atmosphere of the slave
trade: the atmosphere in which it was the fashion to think of men as things.

In the days of the guilds the workman was regarded as a person with
some kind of property or status; the stages by which this character is
restricted to a smaller and smaller part of the working classes, and more and
more of the journeymen and apprentices fall into a permanently inferior
class have been described by historians. In the early nineteenth century the
workers, as a class, were looked upon as so much labour power to be used at
the discretion of, and under conditions imposed by, their masters; not as men
and women who are entitled to some voice in the arrangements of their life
and work. The use of child labour on a vast scale had an important bearing
on the growth of this temper.

The children of the poor were regarded as workers long before the
Industrial Revolution. Locke suggested that they should begin work at
three; Defoe rejoiced to see that in the busy homes of the Yorkshire clothiers
"scarce anything above four years old, but its hands were sufficient for its
own support." The new industrial system provided a great field for the

John L. and Barbara Hammond, *The Rise of Modern Industry* (1925), pp. 194–5, 196–9, 200–1,
210, 211–3, 217–20, 222–4, 226–32. Reprinted by permission of Methuen & Co. Ltd., London.

employment of children, and Pitt himself, speaking in 1796, dwelt on this prospect with a satisfaction strange to modern minds, and disturbing even to some who heard him. One of the most elaborate of all Bentham's fantasies was his scheme for a great series of Industry Houses, 250 in number, each to hold 2,000 persons, for whose work, recreation, education, and marriage most minute regulations were laid down. An advantage he claimed for his system was that it would enable the apprentices to marry at "the earliest period compatible with health," and this was made possible by the employment of children. "And to what would they be indebted for this gentlest of all revolutions? To what, but to economy? Which dreads no longer the multiplication of man, now that she has shown by what secure and unperishable means infant man, a drug at present so much worse than worthless, may be endowed with an indubitable and universal value." Infant man soon became in the new industrial system what he never was in the old, the basis of a complicated economy.

Most children under the old domestic system worked at home under their parents' eyes, but in addition to such children there were workhouse children, who were hired out by overseers to every kind of master or mistress. Little care was taken to see that they were taught a trade or treated with humanity by their employers, and though London magistrates like Fielding did what they could to protect this unhappy class, their state was often a kind of slavery. The number of children on the hands of the London parishes was largely increased in the latter part of the eighteenth century, because an Act of Parliament, passed in 1767 in consequence of the exertions of Jonas Hanway, compelled the London parishes to board out their young children, and to give a bonus to every nurse whose charge survived. Until this time very few parish pauper children grew up to trouble their betters.

The needs of the London workhouses on the one hand, and those of the factory on the other, created a situation painfully like the situation in the West Indies. The Spanish employers in America wanted outside labour, because the supply of native labour was deficient in quantity and quality. The new cotton mills placed on streams in solitary districts were in the same case. The inventions had found immense scope for child labour, and in these districts there were only scattered populations. In the workhouses of large towns there was a quantity of child labour available for employment, that was even more powerless and passive in the hands of a master than the stolen negro, brought from his burning home to the hold of a British slave ship. Of these children it could be said, as it was said of the negroes, that their life at best was a hard one, and that their choice was often the choice between one kind of slavery and another. So the new industry which was to give the English people such immense power in the world borrowed at its origin from the methods of the American settlements.

How closely the apologies for this child serf system followed the apologies for the slave trade can be seen from Romilly's description of a speech made in the House of Commons in 1811. "Mr. Wortley, who spoke on the same side, insisted that, although in the higher ranks of society it was true that to cultivate the affections of children for their family was the source of every virtue, yet that it was not so among the lower orders, and that it was a benefit to take them away from their miserable and depraved parents. He said too that it would be highly injurious to the public to put a stop to the binding of so many apprentices to the cotton manufacturers, as it must necessarily raise the price of labour and enhance the price of cotton manufactured goods."

It was not until 1816 that Parliament would consent to reform this system of transportation. In that year a Bill that had been repeatedly introduced by Mr. Wilbraham Bootle passed both Houses, and it was made illegal for London children to be apprenticed more than forty miles away from their parish. But by this time the problem had changed, for steam-power had superseded water-power and mills could be built in towns; in these towns there were parents who were driven by poverty to send their children to the mills. In the early days of the factory system there had been a prejudice against sending children to the mill, but the hand-loom weaver had been sinking steadily from the beginning of the century into deeper and deeper poverty, and he was no longer able to maintain himself and his family. Sometimes too an adult worker was only given work on condition that he send his child to the mill. Thus the apprentice system was no longer needed. It had carried the factories over the first stage and at the second they could draw on the population of the neighbourhood.

These children, who were commonly called "free-labour children," were employed from a very early age. Most of them were piecers: that is they had to join together or piece the threads broken in the several roving or spinning machines. But there were tasks less skilled than these, and Robert Owen said that many children who were four or five years old were set to pick up waste cotton on the floor. Their hours were those of the apprentice children. They entered the mill gates at five or six in the morning and left them again at seven or eight at night. They had half an hour for breakfast and an hour for dinner, but even during meal hours they were often at work cleaning a standing machine; Fielden calculated that a child following the spinning machine could walk twenty miles in the twelve hours. Oastler was once in the company of a West Indian slave-master and three Bradford Spinners. When the slave-master heard what were the children's hours he declared: "I have always thought myself disgraced by being the owner of slaves, but we never in the West Indies thought it possible for any human being to be so cruel as to require a child of nine years old to work twelve and a half hours a day."

This terrible evil fastened itself on English life as the other fastened itself on the life of the Colonies. Reformers had an uphill struggle to get rid of its worst abuses. Throughout this long struggle the apologies for child labour were precisely the same as the apologies for the slave trade. Cobbett put it in 1833 that the opponents of the Ten Hours Bill had discovered that

England's manufacturing supremacy depended on 30,000 little girls. This was no travesty of their argument. The champions of the slave trade pointed to the £70,000,000 invested in the sugar plantations, to the dependence of our navy on our commerce, and to the dependence of our commerce on the slave trade. This was the argument of Chatham in one generation and Rodney in another. When Fox destroyed the trade in 1806 even Sir Robert Peel complained that we were philosophizing when our looms were idle, and George Rose, that the Americans would take up the trade, and that Manchester, Stockport and Paisley would starve. . . .

The argument for child labour followed the same line. In the one case the interests of Liverpool, in the other those of Lancashire, demanded of the nation that it should accept one evil in order to escape from another. Cardwell, afterwards the famous army reformer, talked of the great capital sunk in the cotton industry and the danger of the blind impulse of humanity. Sir James Graham thought that the Ten Hours Bill would ruin the cotton industry and with it the trade of the country. The cotton industry had taken the place in this argument that had been held by the navy in the earlier controversy. Our population, which had grown so rapidly in the Industrial Revolution, was no longer able to feed itself: the food it bought was paid for by its manufactures: those manufactures depended on capital: capital depended on profits: profits depended on the labour of the boys and girls who enabled the manufacturer to work his mills long enough at a time to repay the cost of the plant and to compete with his foreign rivals. This was the circle in which the nation found its conscience entangled.

The life of man had been regulated before by the needs of a particular order or the pattern of a particular society: the government of king or church or lord had defined narrow limits within which a man was to run his course. The new master was a world force, for this economy could make its profits, so it was believed, where it chose, and when Englishmen rebelled against its rule it would seek its gains and bestow its blessings elsewhere. This way of looking at the new industrial system put man at the mercy of his machines, for if the new power was not made man's servant, it was bound to become his master. If at every point the governing claim was not man's good but the needs of the machine, it was inevitable that man's life and the quality of his civilization should be subordinated to this great system of production.

Nobody could argue that the ordinary worker before the Industrial Revolution was a free man, whether he was a peasant in the country or a journeyman in the town, but the age which watched the change from domestic to factory industry in Lancashire and Yorkshire could see that a great many men and women lost what they had possessed of initiative and choice.

*　　*　　*

What happened at the Industrial Revolution was that all the restraints that the law imposed on workmen in particular industries, were standardized into a general law for the whole of the expanding world of industry, and all the regulations and laws that recognized him as a person with rights were withdrawn or became inoperative. The workman, as we have seen, lost one by one the several Acts of Parliament that gave him protection from his master in this or that industry. His personal liberty was circumscribed by a series of Acts, beginning with the Act of 1719, which made it a crime for him to take his wits and his skills into another country: a law that applied to the artisan but not to the inventor. At the end of the century the masters were given complete control of their workmen, by a Combination Act which went far beyond the Acts against combinations already on the Statute book. By the Combination Act of 1799 any workman who combined with any other workman to seek an improvement in his working conditions was liable to be brought before a single magistrate—it might be his own employer—and sent to prison for three months. This Act, the chief authors of which were Pitt and Wilberforce, was modified next year, when Parliament decided that two magistrates were necessary to form a court, and that a magistrate who was a master in the trade affected should not try offences, but these modifications did not affect in practice the power that the law gave to employers. Under cover of this Act it often happened that a master would threaten his workman with imprisonment or service in the fleet in order to compel him to accept the wages he chose to offer. In 1824 Place and Hume, taking advantage of the reaction from the worst of the panics produced by the French Revolution, managed to carry the repeal of the Combination Laws. Next year, after their repeal had been celebrated by an outburst of strikes, a less stringent law was put in their place. But the view of the new system as a beneficent mechanism which the mass of men must serve with a blind and unquestioning obedience was firmly rooted in the temper of the time, and thus anyone who tried to think of Englishmen in the spirit of Burke's description of a man, found himself strangely out of tune in a world where the workman was refused education, political rights and any voice in the conditions of his employment.

"At Tyldesley," it was said in a pamphlet published during a strike, "they work fourteen hours per day, including the nominal hour for dinner; the door is locked in working hours, except half an hour at tea time; the workpeople are not allowed to send for water to drink, in the hot factory: and even the rain water is locked up, by the master's order, otherwise they would be happy to drink even that." In this mill a shilling fine was inflicted on a spinner found dirty, or found washing, heard whistling or found with his window open in a temperature of 84 degrees. The men who were thrust into this discipline, however hard and bare their lives, had been accustomed to work in their own homes at their own time. The sense of servitude that was impressed on the age by this discipline, by the methods of government, the look of the towns and the absence of choice or initiative in the lives of the mass of the work-people, was strengthened by the spectacle of the new power. "While the engine runs," wrote an observer, "the people must work—

men, women and children yoked together with iron and steam. The animal machine—breakable in the best case, subject to a thousand sources of suffering—is chained fast to the iron machine which knows no suffering and no weariness."

"Two centuries ago not one person in a thousand wore stockings; one century ago not one person in five hundred wore them; now not one person in a thousand is without them." This sentence from *The Results of Machinery* (1831), one of the publications of the Society for the Diffusion of Useful Knowledge, illustrates a feature of the Industrial Revolution that made a profound impression on the imagination of the time. When capital was applied to production on a large scale, it gained its profits by producing in bulk; producing, that is, for mass consumption. Energy and brains were now devoted to satisfying, not the luxurious taste of the classes that were served by the commerce of medieval Europe, but the needs of the poor consumer.

It was natural for the age that witnessed the first triumphs of the new system to worship production for profit. This great addition to the wealth of the world seemed to follow automatically when men were left to acquire at their pleasure. Swift success is a dazzling spectacle, and the new industrial system provided a new miracle every day. . . .

The English people, from the whole tone and cast of its thought and politics, was specially liable to be swept off its balance by this revolution. The positive enthusiasms of the time were for science and progress: for material development and individual liberty. The restraints of custom, tradition and religion had never been so frail over the classes that held power. In the Middle Ages the Church had laid a controlling or checking hand on manners: the Guilds had hampered individual enterprise by a corporate discipline. But the Church of the eighteenth century was merely part of the civil order, without standards, authority or conscience of its own; the Guilds were dead, and their successors stood not for corporate spirit, but for property and nothing else. Thus neither Church nor Guild survived to offer any obstacle to the view that headlong wealth was the sovereign good for society and for the individual, for cities and for men.

This view was powerfully encouraged by the philosophy of confidence which the eighteenth century had substituted for a religion of awe. Medieval religion had watched man's instincts with anxious eyes, as instincts needing to be disciplined, coerced, held fast by Pope and priest; the Puritans, though they gave him different masters, were not less suspicious of the natural man. The new philosophy, on the other hand, regarded man's instincts as the best guide to conduct, and taught that left to himself man so acted as to serve rather than injure the society to which he belonged. Capital was a magical power; man was a benevolent creature. Thus so far as an age lives by a system of belief, this age drew its wisdom from a philosophy that found nothing but good in the new force to which it had submitted.

The state of politics was also congenial to this impulse. Neither Conservative nor Radical offered any distracting or competing motive, for while they disagreed about political and administrative reform, they did not disagree about the advantages of a system under which acquisition and profit-making were unimpeded. If it was the manufacturers who promoted the new system in industry, the landowners were equally active in promoting it on their estates. The most important force in making the English an industrial people was the destruction of the village. Nations that kept the peasant could never be completely absorbed in the new industrial system, and it was the landowner, often of course the new landowner, who had come from the world of finance and industry, who pushed the English peasant out.

England was on the eve of a great expansion of resources, numbers, wealth and power. What were the new towns to be like? What their schools, their pleasures, their houses, their standards of a good life, their plans for cooperation and fellowship? What the fate of the mass of people who did not feel or force their way through the doors thrown open to enterprise? To all these questions the Industrial Revolution gave the same answer: "Ask Capital." And neither Conservative nor Radical, the man defending or the man attacking bad laws and bad customs, thought that answer wrong. But that answer meant that the age had turned aside from making a society in order to make a system of production.

The effect of this concentration is seen in the towns of the age. They were left, like everything else, to the mercy and direction of the spirit of profit. . . .

Yet the Industrial Revolution which had given these men their fortunes had made it much easier to supply the needs of the towns that sprang up beside their great establishments. One of the products of that revolution was gas lighting; the Soho Works were lighted with gas in 1802 to celebrate the Peace of Amiens. Great factories at Manchester and Leeds soon followed the example of Boulton and Watt. Another product was the cheap water-pipe. At the end of the American War English ironmasters were exporting water-pipes to Paris and New York. The Romans had no cheap water-pipes made by the help of mechanical power, but they could supply their towns with clean water, whereas the people of Merthyr Tydfil, their streets echoing by day and night with the clamour of forge and furnace, had to drink whatever the river brought them.

The rage for production had swept England, as the rage for piety had swept the age of the monarchists. And production had taken a form that was intensely isolating; the successful man kept his secrets, tried to find his neighbours' secrets, strove for personal gain, took personal risks, made his way by personal initiative and personal enterprise.

This concentration led to the complete neglect of the most urgent tasks of the age. In the first twenty years of the nineteenth century the population of Manchester increased from 94,000 to 160,000; of Bolton from 29,000 to 50,000; Leeds more than doubled its population between 1801 and 1831; Bradford, which had 23,000 inhabitants in 1831, grew grass in its streets at the end of the eighteenth century. Oldham, which had 38,000 inhabitants in

1821, had three or four hundred in 1760. In the twenty years from 1801 to 1821 the population of Lancashire grew from 672,000 to 1,052,000; in the next twenty years it grew to 1,701,000. The population of Merthyr increased from 7,700 to 35,000 between 1801 and 1841, and that of the two counties of Glamorgan and Monmouth from 126,000 to 305,000. Industry was accumulating dense masses of people into particular districts, where the workman was shut up in melancholy streets, without gardens or orchards. England was passing from a country to a town life, as she passed from a peasant to an industrial civilization. What this meant is clear if we compare the state of the towns as revealed in the health statistics, with that of the country districts. In 1757 Dr. Percival put the death-rate for Manchester at 1 in 25, for Liverpool at 1 in 27. In Monton, a few miles from Manchester, the ratio was at that time 1 in 68, at Horwich, between Bolton and Chorley, 1 in 66, at Darwen, three miles from Blackburn, 1 in 56. The Industrial Revolution was to spread the conditions of town life over places like Monton, Horwich and Darwen.

The problem of arranging and controlling the expansion of the towns was thus the most urgent of the problems created by the Industrial Revolution. Its importance was illustrated by a picture of some cottages near Preston published by the Health of Towns Commission in 1844. These cottages stood in two rows, separated by little back yards, with an open sewer running the whole length. The picture was given as an example of dangerous and disgusting drainage. But this is not its chief significance. One would suppose that these huddled cottages, without gardens of any kind, were built in a crowded town, where not an inch of space was available for amenities. They were in fact in the open country. Clearly then there was more here than a problem of drainage, for if it was left to private enterprise to develop this district, under the guidance of an uncontrolled sense for profit, these rows would spring up all round, and Preston would have another slum on her hands. This is what happened in the new industrial districts. When the Health of Towns Commission investigated towns like Manchester, they were told that the worst evils were not the evils of the past, for new Manchester was reproducing the slums and alleys of the old, and spreading them, of course, over a far wider surface. Of no other problem was it so true that neglect by one generation tied the hands and the mind of the next. . . .

The importance of preserving amenities, footpaths, and something of the look of the country was impressed on Parliament. The most significant comment of the neglect of these proposals is to be found in the recurring complaint that runs through all the Reports on Health and Housing that were issued in the nineteenth century. Town planning never found its way into an Act of Parliament until the twentieth century, and back-to-back houses (made illegal in 1909) were built in great numbers two generations after Normanby's Bill had proposed to forbid them. The Commission which sat in 1867 found in existence the main evils that were revealed by the Committee of 1840; the Commission of 1884 found in existence the main evils that had been revealed by the Commission of 1867. In many towns the

death-rate was higher in 1867 than in 1842, and Cross, speaking as Home
Secretary in 1871, could match the terrible revelations by which Chadwick
had tried to rouse the indignation and fear of the Parliaments of Melbourne
and Peel.

Before each Commission the large towns disclosed the same difficulties.
The law did not enable them to control expansion, or to prevent the creation
on their circumference of the evils they were trying to suppress at the centre.
The Committee of 1840 had pointed out that back-to-back houses were being
introduced into towns that had been free from them. Town Clerks told the
Commission of 1867 that whole streets were still being built on "a foundation
composed of old sweepings, refuse from factories, old buildings and other
objectionable matter." Parliament passed Public Health Acts and set up
authorities with sharply limited powers, but the fatal blindness to the character of the problem, as a problem in the organization and planning of town
life, which marked the early phases of the Industrial Revolution, persisted.
England learnt sooner than other countries how to cleanse her towns, but
towns still continued to grow at the pleasure of the profit seeker. Each
generation looked wistfully back to its predecessor as living in a time when
the evil was still manageable, and over the reforms of the century could be
inscribed the motto "the Clock that always loses." For the creed of the first
age of the Industrial Revolution, that the needs of production must regulate
the conditions of life, and that the incidence of profits must decide in what
kind of town, in what kind of streets, and in what kind of houses a nation
shall find its home, had cast its melancholy fatalism over the mind of the
generations that followed. The trouble was not merely that the evil was
greater when a town had a quarter of a million of inhabitants instead of a
hundred thousand. It was that men still saw with the eyes of their grandfa-
thers, and that they were busy polishing the life of the slum, when a race that
was free and vigorous in its mind could have put an end to it. With the
consequences and the traditions of this neglect industrial civilization is still
fighting an up-hill battle.

The other task that became immensely more important with the Industrial Revolution was the task of education. Adam Smith had pointed out that
the division of labour, though good for production, was bad for the mind of
the labourer. Men, women and children lost range, diversity and incentive in
their work, when that work was simplified to a single process, or a monoto-
nous routine. Life was more versatile and interesting when craftsmanship
was combined with agriculture. Under the new system a boy or youth learnt
one process and one process only; a great part of his mind was never
exercised; many of his faculties remained idle and undeveloped. Moreover,
apprenticeship was declining, and thus an important method of education
was passing out of fashion.

Nor were these the only reasons why popular education was needed
more urgently in this than in previous ages. Men learn from their leisure as

well as from their work. Now the common life of the time was singularly wanting in inspiration, comparing in this respect unfavourably with the life of the ancient or that of the medieval world. The Greeks and the Romans put a great deal of beauty into their public buildings; they made provision, in some cases barbarous provision, for public amusement; they did not isolate art and pleasure for the delight of a small class. Life in Manchester or Merthyr was very different. Mr. and Mrs. Webb, who have described the work of the several bodies of Improvement Commissioners at this time, remark that even the most energetic among them made no provision for parks, open spaces, libraries, picture galleries, museums, baths, or any kind of education. The workmen put it that their sports had been converted into crimes, and their holidays into fast days. Rich men in the Roman Empire spent their money on things that were for common enjoyment as rich men in the Middle Ages spent their money on things that were for common salvation. Pliny gave to his native Como, a library, a school endowment, a foundation for the nurture of poor children and a Temple of Ceres with spacious colonnades to shelter the traders who visited the great fair. The wealthy Herodes Atticus, tutor of Marcus Aurelius, gave a theatre to Athens with a roof of cedar to hold 6,000 persons, another theatre to Corinth, and a race-course to Delphi. Such gifts were common in the days of the Antonines. But in the England of the early Industrial Revolution all diversions were regarded as wrong, because it was believed that successful production demanded long hours, a bare life, a mind without temptation to think or to remember, to look before or behind. Some Lancashire magistrates used to refuse on this ground to license public-houses where concerts were held. Long hours did not begin with the Industrial Revolution, but in the Middle Ages the monotony of industrial work was broken for the journeyman by frequent holidays, saints' days and festivals; for medieval Europe, like Rome, gave some place in common life to the satisfaction of the imagination and the senses.

Perhaps nothing served so directly to embitter the relations of class in the Industrial Revolution as this fashionable view, that the less amusement the worker had, the better. The love of amusement has a place of special significance in the English character. If the English workman stints himself for his holiday week at Blackpool, as the Scottish peasant stints himself to send his son into the Ministry, or the Irish or French peasant stints himself to own a little property, it is not merely because he sets his holiday high among the enjoyments of life. The satisfaction of this desire is connected with his self-respect. The football field and the holiday resort represent a world in which the poor man feels himself the equal of the rich: a corner of life in which he has not bargained away any rights or liberties. It might be said of the early Radicals, that they sought to extend to his view of politics, and of the early Socialists, that they sought to extend to his views of property, the spirit that ruled the workman's outlook on his pleasures: that they sought to make him resent in those spheres the inequalities he was so quick to resent, when employer or magistrate tried to keep from him amusements that other classes enjoyed.

The need for popular education became in these circumstances specially urgent. The reading of print is one way of using and exercising the mind, and its value at any moment depends on circumstances. In the days of pageants and spectacles, when story-tellers went from village to village, when pedlars and pilgrims brought tales of adventure or war or the habits of foreign countries, a man might be unable to read or write, and yet take a share in the culture of the time. Buildings, plays, music, these may be greater influences on the mind than book or pamphlet or newspaper. But the youth of the early nineteenth century who found no scope for initiative or experiment or design in his work, found no stimulus or education for his fancy from the spectacles and amusements provided for his recreation. Science was improving the mechanical contrivances of life, but the arts of life were in decline. To take advantage of these improvements, the power to read and write was essential. In a world depending on newspapers, the man who cannot read lives in the darkest exile; when the factory was taking the place of the craft, the newspaper the place of the pageant, illiteracy was the worst disfranchisement a man could suffer.

Horner, reporting in 1839 that a population of over a hundred thousand persons in a district of Lancashire comprising Oldham and Ashton was without a single public day-school for poor scholars, the Commissioner who said of South Wales in 1842 that not one grown male in fifty could read, both spoke of an age in which the story-teller had left the village, and the apprenticeship system was leaving the town. Adam Smith had argued that as the division of labour deprived the worker of opportunities of training his mind, the State ought to provide opportunities by public education. The ruling class argued, on the contrary, that with the new methods of specialization, industry could not spare a single hour for the needs of the men who served it. In such a system education had no place. The great majority of the ruling class believed, as one of them put it, that the question to ask was not whether education would develop a child's faculties for happiness and citizenship, but whether it "would make him a good servant in agriculture and other laborious employments to which his rank in society had destined him."

Thus England asked for profits and received profits. Everything turned to profit. The towns had their profitable dirt, their profitable smoke, their profitable slums, their profitable disorder, their profitable ignorance, their profitable despair. The curse of Midas was on this society: on its corporate life, on its common mind, on the decisive and impatient step it had taken from the peasant to the industrial age. For the new town was not a home where man could find beauty, happiness, leisure, learning, religion—the influences that civilize outlook and habit; but a bare and desolate place, without colour, air or laughter, where man, woman and child worked, ate and slept. This was to be the lot of the mass of mankind: this the sullen rhythm of their lives. The new factories and the new furnaces were like the Pyramids, telling of man's enslavement, rather than of his power, casting their long shadow over the society that took such pride in them.

The foremost proponent of the necessity for revising the traditional accounts of the Industrial Revolution is T. S. Ashton, Professor Emeritus of Economic History at the University of London.

FROM *The Treatment of Capitalism by Historians*

BY T. S. ASHTON

THE STUDENT OF ENGLISH ECONOMIC HISTORY is fortunate in having at his disposal the reports of a long series of Royal Commissions and Committees of Inquiry beginning in the eighteenth century but reaching full stream in the 1830's, 1840's, and 1850's. These reports are one of the glories of the early Victorian age. They signalized a quickening of social conscience, a sensitiveness to distress, that had not been evident in any other period or in any other country. Scores of massive folios provided statistical and verbal evidence that all was not well with large numbers of the people of England and called the attention of legislators and the reading public to the need for reform. The economic historians of the succeeding generations could do no other than draw on their findings; and scholarship, no less than society, benefited. There was, however, loss as well as gain. A picture of the economic system constructed from Blue Books dealing with social grievances, and not with the normal processes of economic development, was bound to be one-sided. It is such a picture of early Victorian society that has become fixed in the minds of popular writers. . . . A careful reading of the reports would, indeed, lead to the conclusion that much that was wrong was the result of laws, customs, habits, and forms of organization that belonged to earlier periods and were rapidly becoming obsolete. It would have brought home to the mind that it was not among the factory employees but among the domestic workers, whose traditions and methods were those of the eighteenth century, that earnings were at their lowest. It would have provided evidence that it was not in the large establishments making use of steam

Thomas S. Ashton, "The Treatment of Capitalism by Historians," reprinted from *Capitalism and the Historians,* edited by F. A. Hayek, by permission of The University of Chicago Press. Copyright 1954 by The University of Chicago.

power but in the garret or cellar workshops that conditions of employment were at their worst. It would have led to the conclusion that it was not in the growing manufacturing towns or the developing coal fields but in re- mote villages and the countryside that restrictions on personal freedom and the evils of truck were most marked. But few had the patience to go carefully through these massive volumes. It was so much easier to pick out the more sensational evidences of distress and work them into a dramatic story of ex- ploitation. The result has been that a generation that had the enterprise and industry to assemble the facts, the honesty to reveal them, and the energy to set about the task of reform has been held up to obloquy as the author, not of the Blue Books, but of the evils themselves. Conditions in the mills and the factory town were so bad, it seemed, that there must have been deteriora- tion; . . . and, since the supposed deterioration had taken place at a time when machinery had increased, the machines, and those who owned them, must have been responsible.

At the same time the romantic revival in literature led to an idyllic view of the life of the peasant. The idea that agriculture is the only natural and healthy activity for human beings has persisted, and indeed spread, as more of us have escaped from the curse of Adam—or, as the tedious phrase goes, "become divorced from the soil." A year ago an examinee remarked pro- foundly that "in earlier centuries agriculture was widespread in England" but added sorrowfully, "Today it is confined to the rural areas." There was a similar idealization of the condition of the domestic worker, who had taken only the first step in the proceedings for divorce. Bear with me while I read some passages with which Friedrich Engels (who is usually acclaimed a realist) opens his account of *The Condition of the Working Classes in England in 1844.* It is, of course, based on the writings of the Reverend Philip Gaskell, whose earnestness and honesty are not in doubt, but whose mind had not been confused by any study of history. Engels' book opens with the declaration that "the history of the proletariat in England begins with the invention of the steam-engine and of machinery for working cotton." Before their time, he continues,

> the workers vegetated throughout a passably comfortable existence, lead- ing a righteous and peaceful life in all piety and probity; and their material condition was far better than that of their successors. They did not need to overwork; they did no more than they chose to do, and yet earned what they needed. They had leisure for healthful work in garden or field, work which, in itself, was recreation for them, and they could take part beside in the recreation and games of their neighbours, and all these games—bowling, cricket, football, etc. contributed to their physical health and vigour. They were, for the most part, strong, well-built people, in whose physique little or no difference from that of their peasant neighbours was discoverable. Their children grew up in fresh country air, and, if they could help their parents at work, it was only

occasionally; while of eight or twelve hours work for them there was no question.

It is difficult to say whether this or the lurid picture of the lives of the grandchildren of these people presented in later pages of the book is more completely at variance with the facts. Engels had no doubt whatsoever as to the cause of the deterioration in the condition of labor. "The proletariat," he repeats, "was called into existence by the introduction of machinery." "The consequences of improvement in machinery under our present social conditions," he asserts, "are, for the working-man, solely injurious, and often in the highest degree oppressive. Every new advance brings with it loss of employment, want and suffering."

Engels has had many disciples, even among those who do not accept the historical materialism of Marx, with which such views are generally connected. Hostility to the machine is associated with hostility to its products and, indeed, to all innovation in consumption. One of the outstanding accomplishments of the new industrial age is to be seen in the greatly increased supply and variety of fabrics offered on the market. Yet the changes in dress are taken as evidence of growing poverty: "The clothing of the working-people in a majority of cases," Engels declares, "is in a very bad condition. The material used for it is not of the best adapted. Wool and linen have almost vanished from the wardrobes of both sexes, and cotton has taken their place. Skirts are made of bleached or coloured cotton goods, and woollen petticoats are rarely to be seen on the wash-line." The truth is that they never had been greatly displayed on the wash line, for woolen goods are liable to shrink. The workers of earlier periods had to make their garments last (second or third hand as many of these were), and soap and water were inimical to the life of clothing. The new, cheap textiles may not have been as hard-wearing as broadcloth, but they were more abundant; and the fact that they could be washed without suffering harm had a bearing, if not on their own life, at least on the lives of those who wore them.

The same hostility is shown to innovation in food and drink. Generations of writers have followed William Cobbett in his hatred of tea. One would have thought that the enormous increase in consumption between the beginning of the eighteenth and the middle of the nineteenth century was one element in a rising standard of comfort; but only a few years ago Professor Parkinson asserted that it was "growing poverty" that made tea increasingly essential to the lower classes as ale was put beyond their means. (This, I may add, unfortunately meant that they were forced to consume sugar, and one must suppose that this practice also led to a fall in the standard of living.) Similarly, Dr. Salaman has recently assured us that the introduction of the potato into the diet of the workers at this time was a factor detrimental to health and that it enabled the employers to force down the level of wages—which, it is well known, is always determined by the minimum of food required for subsistence.

Very gradually those who held to these pessimistic views of the effects of industrial change have been forced to yield ground. The painstaking researches of Bowley and Wood have shown that over most of this period, and later, the course of real wages was upward. The proof is not at all easy, for it is clear that there were sections of the working classes of whom it was emphatically not true. In the first half of the nineteenth century the population of England was growing, partly because of natural increase, partly as the result of the influx of Irish. For those endowed with little or no skill, marginal productivity, and hence earnings, remained low. A large part of their incomes was spent on commodities (mainly food, drink, and housing), the cost of which had hardly been affected by technical development. That is why so many of the economists, like McCulloch and Mill, were themselves dubious about the beneficial nature of the industrial system. There were, however, large and growing sections of skilled and better-paid workers whose money incomes were rising and who had a substantial margin to spend on the products of the machine, the costs of which were falling progressively. The controversy really rests on which of the groups was increasing most. Generally it is now agreed that for the majority the gain in real wages was substantial.

But this does not dispose of the controversy. Real earnings might have risen, it was said, but it was the quality of life and not the quantity of goods consumed that mattered. In particular, it was the evil conditions of housing and the insanitary conditions of the towns that were called as evidence that the circumstances of labor had worsened. "Everything which here arouses horror and indignation," wrote Engels of Manchester in 1844, "is of recent origin, belongs to the industrial epoch"—and the reader is left to infer that the equally repulsive features of cities like Dublin and Edinburgh, which were scarcely touched by the new industry, were, somehow or other, also the product of the machine.

This is the legend that has spread round the world and has determined the attitude of millions of men and women to labor-saving devices and to those who own them. Indians and Chinese, Egyptians and Negroes, to whose fellow-countrymen today the dwellings of the English of the mid-nineteenth century would be wealth indeed, solemnly declare, in the scripts I have to read, that the English workers were living in conditions unworthy of beasts. They write with indignation about the inefficiency of the sanitation and the absence of civic amenities—the very nature of which is still unknown to the urban workers of a large part of the earth.

Now, no one who has read the reports of the Committee on the Sanitary Condition of the Working Classes of 1842 or that of the Commission on the Health of Towns of 1844 can doubt that the state of affairs was, from the point of view of modern Western civilization, deplorable. But, equally, no one who has read Dorothy George's account of living conditions in London in the eighteenth century can be sure that they had deteriorated. Dr. George herself believes that they had improved, and Clapham declared that the

English towns of the mid-century were "less crowded than the great towns of other countries and not, universally, more insanitary." The question I wish to raise, however, is that of responsibility. Engels, as we have seen, attributed the evils to the machine; others are no less emphatic in attributing them to the Industrial Revolution, which comes to much the same thing. No historian, as far as I know, has looked at the problem through the eyes of those who had the task of building and maintaining the towns.

There were two main aspects: the supply of houses in relation to the demand and the technical matters of drainage, sanitation, and ventilation. In the early nineteenth century, according to one of these scripts, "the workers were pressed into back-to-back houses, like sardines in a rabbit warren." Many of the houses were certainly unsubstantial and insanitary, and for this it is usual to blame the industrialist who put them up, a man commonly spoken of as the jerry-builder. I had often wondered who this man was. When I was young, the parson of the church I attended once preached a sermon on Jerry, who, he asserted with complete conviction, was at that very moment burning in hell for his crimes. I have searched for records of him, but in vain. It appears from Weekley's *Etymological Dictionary of Modern English* that "jerry" is a corruption of "jury"—a word of nautical origin applied to any part of a ship contrived for temporary use, as in "jury mast" and "jury rig," and extended to other things, such as "jury leg" for "wooden leg." "Jerry," then, means temporary, or inferior, or makeshift; and no doubt other uses of the word as a makeshift in an emergency will come to the mind. According to Partridge's *Dictionary of Slang and Unconventional English,* it was first used in Liverpool about 1830. The place and time are significant. Liverpool was the port for the rapidly developing industrial area of southeastern Lancashire; it was the chief gate of entry for the swarms of Irish immigrants. It was probably here that the pressure of population on the supplies of accommodation was most acute. Houses were run up rapidly, and many of them were flimsy structures, the outer walls of which were only 4½ inches in thickness. On December 5, 1822, some of them, along with many buildings elsewhere, were blown down in a great storm that swept over the British Isles; and in February, 1823, the grand jury at Liverpool called the attention of the magistrates "to the dreadful effects of the late storm . . . in consequence of the modern insecure mode of building." A year later the same body referred again to "the slight and dangerous mode of erecting dwelling houses now practised in this town and neighbourhood" and asked for steps to be taken "to procure a Legislative enactment, which might empower a proper Officer carefully to survey every building hereafter to be erected, and in case of insecurity to cause the danger to be removed."

The sudden collapse of buildings was no new experience. In 1738 Samuel Johnson had written of London as a place where "falling houses thunder on your head"; and, to give a specific instance, in 1796 two houses fell, burying sixteen people, in Houghton Street, where the concrete buildings of the School of Economics now stand. The chief trouble seems to have been the use of inferior material, such as ashes and street sweepings, in the making of bricks and the unsubstantial walls erected whenever the building lease was for only a short run of years. It would appear from the Liverpool evidence, however, that matters had taken a turn for the worse in the early 1820's; and complaints of inferior building in other quarters reinforce the belief. The explanation is not far to seek. It lies in the fact that the early twenties saw a revival of housebuilding after a long period of suspension (or, at best, feeble activity) during nearly a quarter of a century of war and that this revival took place in circumstances when building costs had been raised to an inordinate height.

It is necessary to take account of the organization of the industry. The typical builder was a man of small means, a bricklayer or a carpenter who bought a small plot of land, carried out himself only a single operation, such as that of laying the bricks, and employed craftsmen on contract for the other processes of construction. By the middle of the nineteenth century, it is true, large-scale firms were growing up, controlled by men like Thomas Cubitt, but these were concerned with the erection of public buildings or mansions and not with the dwellings of the poor. The jerry-builders were not, in the usual sense of the word, capitalists, but workingmen. Says Chadwick's *Report* of 1842:

> In the rural districts, the worst of the new cottages are those erected on the borders of commons by the labourers themselves. In manufacturing districts, the tenements erected by building clubs and by speculating builders of the class of workmen, are frequently the subject of complaint, as being the least substantial and the most destitute of proper accommodation. The only conspicuous instances of improved residences found in the rural districts are those which have been erected by opulent and benevolent landlords for the accommodation of the labourers on their own estates: and in the manufacturing districts, those erected by wealthy manufacturers for the accommodation of their own workpeople.

In Liverpool the builders of so-called "slop houses," or scamped houses, were usually Welshmen, drawn largely from the quarrymen of Caernarvonshire. They were backed by attorneys who had land to dispose of on lease but were not themselves willing to become builders. They bought their materials, which were of a cheap and shoddy type, on three months' credit. They tended to employ a high proportion of apprentices, and so, it was said, workmanship was of low quality. They needed credit at every stage: to obtain the building lease, to purchase the materials, and to meet the claims of the joiners, plasterers, slaters, plumbers, painters, etc., who performed their special tasks as contractors or subcontractors. The price of money was an important element in building costs. Under the operation of the usury laws it was illegal to offer, or demand, more than 5 per cent, and this meant that, at times when the state itself was offering 4½ or more per cent, it was impossible for the builders to obtain loans at all. By allowing the rate of interest to rise to 4½ or 5 per cent on the public debt, and prohibiting the industrialist from offering more, the state had been successful in damping down the activities of the builders for more than twenty years and so had deflected to itself the resources of men and materials required for the prosecution of the war against Napoleon. After 1815 the rate of interest fell tardily; it was not until the early twenties that the builders could resume operations. They were faced with a demand that had swollen enormously as the result of a vast increase of population, which now included an abnormally large number of young adults seeking homes of their own.

They were faced also by an enormous increase in costs. In 1821, according to Silberling's index number, wholesale prices in general stood about 20 per cent above the level of the year 1788. In the same period the price of building materials had risen far more: bricks and wainscot had doubled; deals had risen by 60 per cent and lead by 58 per cent. The wages of craftsmen and laborers had gone up by anything from 80 to 100 per cent. The costs of a large number of specific operations are given annually in the *Builders' Price Books* published in London. They show an increase in the cost of plain brickwork of 120 per cent. Oak for building purposes had gone up by 150 per cent, and fir by no less than 237 per cent. The cost of common painting had doubled, and that of glazing with crown glass had increased by 140 per cent.

It was not, in the main, the producer of materials who was responsible. During the war the duties levied by the state on bricks and tiles, stone, slate, and wallpaper had increased enormously. At this time the cost of timber was the chief element in the total cost of building materials, amounting, according to one estimate, to fully a half of the whole. Almost prohibitive duties had been laid on the supplies of timber and deals from the Baltic, and the builders of working-class houses had to make use of what were generally said to be inferior woods, brought at great cost across the Atlantic from Canada. Joseph Hume declared, in 1850, that, if the duties on bricks and timber were removed, a cottage which cost £60 to build, as things were, could be put up for £40.

*   *   *

In the years that followed the long war, then, the builders had the task of making up arrears of housing and of meeting the needs of a rapidly growing population. They were handicapped by costs, a large part of which arose from fiscal exactions. The expenses of occupying a house were loaded with heavy local burdens, and so the net rent that most workingmen could afford to pay was reduced. In these circumstances, if the relatively poor were to be housed at all, the buildings were bound to be smaller, less substantial, and less well provided with amenities than could be desired. It was emphatically not the machine, not the Industrial Revolution, not even the speculative bricklayer or carpenter that was at fault. Few builders seem to have made fortunes, and the incidence of bankruptcy was high. The fundamental problem was the shortage of houses. Those who blame the jerry-builder remind one of the parson, referred to by Edwin Cannan, who used to upbraid the assembled worshipers for the poor attendance at church.

Stress has rightly been laid by many writers on the inadequacy of the provisions for safeguarding the public against overcrowding of houses on limited sites. But London, Manchester, and other large towns had had their Building Acts for generations, and no one who has looked at the *Builders' Price Books* can possibly believe that Londoners suffered from a deficiency of regulations. Mr. John Summerson, indeed, has suggested that the depressing monotony of the newer streets of the capital were the direct result, not, as is often assumed, of free enterprise, but of the provisions of what the builders called the Black Act of 1774—a measure that runs to about thirty-five thousand words. It is true that what was uppermost in the minds of those who framed this act was the avoidance of fire. But some writers like the Webbs (as Redford has shown) have done less than justice to the work of the early organs of local government in such matters as the paving, lighting, and cleaning of streets. If more was not done, the fault did not rest on the builders. Thomas Cubitt told the House of Commons that he would not allow a house to be built anywhere unless it could be shown that there was a good drainage and a good way to get rid of water. "I think there should be a public officer paid at the public expense, who should be responsible for that." If the towns were ridden with disease, some at least of the responsibility lay with legislators who, by taxing windows, put a price on light and air and, by taxing bricks and tiles, discouraged the construction of drains and sewers. Those who dwell on the horrors that arose from the fact that the products of the sewers often got mixed up with the drinking water, and attribute this, as all other horrors, to the Industrial Revolution, should be reminded of the obvious fact that without the iron pipe, which was one of the products of that revolution, the problem of enabling people to live a healthy life together in towns could never have been solved.

If my first complaint against commonly accepted views of the economic developments of the nineteenth century is concerned with their pessimism, my second is that they are not informed by any glimmering of economic sense. In the generation of Adam Smith and his immediate successors many treatises appeared dealing with the history of commerce, industry, coinage, public revenue, population, and pauperism. Those who wrote them—men like Anderson, Macpherson, Chalmers, Colquhoun, Lord Liverpool, Sinclair, Eden, Malthus, and Tooke—were either themselves economists or at least were interested in the things that were the concern of Adam Smith, Ricardo, and Mill. There were, it is true, many rebels, on both the right and the left, against the doctrines propounded by the economists; but few of these, it so happened, were historically minded. There was, therefore, no sharply defined cleavage between history and theory. In the second half of the nineteenth century, however, a wide breach appeared. How far it was due to the direct influence of the writings of Marx and Engels, how far to the rise of the Historical School of economists in Germany, and how far to the fact that the English economic historians, following Toynbee, were primarily social reformers, I must not stay to discuss. There can be no doubt, however, that the tendency was to write the story in other than economic terms. A whole series of labels was introduced to indicate what were believed to be the dominant characteristics of successive periods of time, and most of these were political rather than economic in connotation. The arresting phrase, the "Industrial Revolution," was coined (as Miss Bezanson has shown) not by English industrialists or economists but by French writers of the late eighteenth century, under the spell of their own great political ferment. It was seized upon by Engels and Marx and was used by Arnold Toynbee as the title of his pioneer work. It may be questioned whether it has not now outlived its usefulness, for it has tended to support the view that the introduction of large-scale production was catastrophic, rather than beneficial, in its effects. Even more unfortunate, I would urge, has been the intrusion into economic history of another phrase of political intent, struck at the same mint but at an even earlier period. Professor Macgregor has traced back the term "laissez faire" to 1755, when it was first used by the Marquis d'Argenson as both a political and an economic principle. He has charted its curious evolution from the time when it meant noninterference with industry to its use, in 1907, by Alfred Marshall to mean "let the State be up and doing." In view of the dubiety of its intention, it is perhaps not to be wondered at that it should have been fastened by some onto a period of English history that is known to others as the Age of Reform—again a phrase drawn from the vocabulary of politics and not of economics. One could not feel too harshly, therefore, about the candidate who declared that "about the year 1900 men turned their backs on laissez-faire and began to do things for themselves." The title of a work written by Mr. Fisher Unwin in 1904 has fastened on the decade that saw the railway boom and the repeal of the Corn Laws the stigma of "the hungry forties," and only the other day a magazine called *Womanfare* referred to the decade before the recent war as "the hungry thirties." A legend is growing up that the years 1930–39 were marked throughout by misery. In the next generation "the hungry thirties" may be common form.

For two generations economic historians have shirked economic questions or have dealt with them superficially. They have never made up their minds on such elementary matters as to whether it is abundance or scarcity that is to be sought, but generally it is restrictionism they favor. The efforts of Lancashire to provide cheap cottons for people who had previously gone seminaked is acknowledged only in a sentence to the effect that "the bones of the cotton weavers whitened the plains of India." In the same elementary textbook I am told that the tax on imports of wheat led to poverty and distress in the first half of the nineteenth century and that the absence of such a tax to act as a dam against the flood of cheap wheat that poured across the Atlantic was the prime cause of the poverty and distress of the later decades of the century—the period so unhappily known as the Great Depression. Some economic historians have written chapters designed to answer such questions as to whether trade arises from industry or industry from trade, whether transport develops markets or markets give occasion for transport. They have concerned themselves with inquiries as to where the demand comes from that makes production possible. Whenever a real problem is encountered, it is passed over with some such comment as that "a crisis arose" or that "speculation became rife," though why or what nature is rarely disclosed. And, when details are given, logic is often thrown to the winds. In explaining the French depression of 1846, Professor Clough declares that "reduced agricultural production lowered the purchasing power of the farmers, and the high cost of living prevented the industrial population from buying much else than food." This surely is a case of making the worst of both worlds. It has often been said that, at least before Keynes, the economic theorist moved in a world of abstractions and had nothing worth while to offer the historian. But, if only historians had pondered a little on marginal analysis, they would have been saved from such foolish assertions as that trade can arise only when there is a surplus or that investment abroad takes place only when the capital market at home is sated. Ignorance of the elements of economic theory led historians to give political interpretations to every favorable trend. In scores of books the improvement in conditions of labor in the nineteenth century has been attributed to factory legislation; in hardly any is it pointed out that rising productivity of male labor had something to do with the decline of the number of children exploited in the factories or the number of women degraded in the mines. Until Professor Rostow wrote his work on the *British Economy of the Nineteenth Century* in 1948, there had been scarcely any discussion by historians of the relation between investment and earnings.

No one has laid more stress on the need for theory in the writing of history than Sombart. "Facts are like beads," he declares; "they require a string to hold them together. . . . No theory—no history." It is to be deplored that he found his own theory, not in the writings of the economists of his day, but in those of Karl Marx; for, although later he reacted strongly against the interpretations of Marx, his writings have led large numbers of historians in Germany, Britain, and the United States to thread their facts on a Marxist string. In particular, everything that has happened, since the early Middle Ages, is explained in terms of capitalism—a term if not coined at least given wide currency by Marx. Marx, of course, associated it with exploitation. Sombart used it to mean a system of production differing from the handicraft system by reason of the fact that the means of production are owned by a class distinct from the workers—a class whose motive is profit and whose methods are rational, as opposed to the traditional methods, of the handicraftsmen. Above all, he stressed the capitalist spirit. Other elements, such as that innovations in the system are carried out by borrowed money, or credit, have been added by later writers like Schumpeter. But nearly all agree that capitalism implies the existence of a rational technique, a proletariat that sells its labor (and not the product of its labor), and a class of capitalists whose aim is unlimited profit. The assumption is that at some stage of human history—perhaps in the eleventh century A.D.—men became, for the first time, rational and acquisitive. The main business of the economic historians who followed Sombart was to trace the origins of rationality and acquisitiveness. It was what they called the "genetic approach" to the problem of capitalism.

A thousand years is an unmanageably long period, and so capitalism had to be presented as a series of stages—the epochs, respectively, of early, full, and late capitalism, or of mercantile capitalism, industrial capitalism, finance capitalism, and state capitalism. It is admitted, of course, by those who make use of these categories that there is overlapping: that the late stage of one epoch is the early (or, as they say, the emergent) stage of the next. But to teach economic history in this way—to suggest that commerce, industry, finance, and state control are *successive* dominant forces—is to hide from the student, I suggest, the interaction and interdependence of all these at every period of time. It is bad economics.

Those who write so tend to torture the facts. It is part of the legend that the dominant form of organization under industrial capitalism, the factory, arose out of the demands, not of ordinary people, but of the rich and the rulers. Let me quote Professor Nussbaum here. "In personal terms," he says, "it was the interests of the princes [the state] and of the industrialists; in impersonal terms, war and luxury favoured—one might almost say, caused—the development of the factory system." To support this monstrous thesis, he gives a list of the capitalized industries about the year 1800. It includes "sugar, chocolate, lace, embroidery, novelties, tapestries, mirrors, porcelains, jewellery, watches and book printing." All I can say is that, apart from that of sugar, I cannot find a single instance of the production of any one of these things in a factory in England at this time. Nussbaum admits that cotton clothes "offered a field for almost exclusively capitalistic organisation" but says that this was because they were "at first and for a long time luxury goods." Apparently he thinks Arkwright and his fellows were making fine muslins and cambrics for royal courts and not calicoes for English workers and the peasants of India. But this legend about war and luxury is too absurd to need refutation by anyone who has taken the trouble to glance at the records of the first generation of factory masters in England.

FROM *The Industrial Revolution* BY T. S. ASHTON

MUCH HAS BEEN WRITTEN about the effects of the industrial revolution on the workers. Some, impressed by the lot of those who went down in

T. S. Ashton, *The Industrial Revolution 1760–1830* (1948), pp. 157–61. Reprinted by permission of Oxford University Press, London.

the struggle against the machine, have declared that technological change brought little but misery and poverty, and a statistician of repute has set on record his opinion that by the early years of the nineteenth century the standard of life of the British worker had been forced down to Asiatic levels. Mr. Colin Clark can hardly have looked at the statistics which more than a generation of research has produced. The careful studies of Mrs. Gilboy indicate that, over the eighteenth century, the material well-being of the labourer in the woollen area of the South-West had, indeed, fallen, but that the lot of his fellow in the textile region of the North had steadily improved, and that the labourer of London more than held his own. It is true that the rise of prices after 1793 made many humble people poorer. But before the end of the war (as Professor Silberling has shown) industrial wages in England caught up with retail prices, and in the 'twenties the gain was pronounced. In 1831 the cost of living was 11 per cent higher than in 1790, but over this span of time urban wages had increased, it appears, by no less than 43 per cent.

It would have been strange, indeed, if the industrial revolution had simply made the rich richer and the poor poorer. For the commodities to which it gave rise were not, in general, luxuries, but necessaries and capital goods. The tardiness with which the last of these yielded their fruit to the consumer has already been explained. But by the 'twenties the effects of the war were passing away and the cottons and woollens, and food and drink, which now became available, were consumed not by the few, but by the masses. Some of the products of the factories and ironworks were sent abroad, but the return cargoes did not consist, in the main, of wines and silks, but of sugar, grain, coffee, and tea for the people at large. Much has been made of the suggestion that the prices of the things Britain exported fell more rapidly than those of the things she brought back: there was no revolution to reduce costs in overseas agriculture; and British lending abroad may also have helped to give the terms of trade an unfavourable turn. But, though such influences may explain why, in the 'thirties and 'forties, real wages were lower than might have been expected, they had little effect, it would seem, between 1815 and 1830. The diet of the worker almost certainly improved: there was a substitution of "flower of wheat" for rye and oatmeal; and meat, which had been a rarity, became, with potatoes, the staple dish on the artisan's table. Not all the coal raised from the pits went to feed the furnaces and steam-engines: a warm hearth and a hot meal were of no small consequence to the man who came home wet from the fields.

In 1802 George Chalmers remarked that the laborious classes were "too wealthy to covet the pittance of the soldier, or too independent to court the dangers of the sailor." There were, true enough, many vagrants and paupers, but, even before the new Poor Law came in, the hordes of the "indigent and distressed" had probably shrunk. Hours of labour were long, and holidays few; there is a mass of evidence that employment in factories was harmful to the health and morals of the young. A leading politician has recently spoken of the "mechanized horrors of the industrial revolution," and there can be little doubt that the deeper mines and more complicated machines brought new risks of mutilation and death. But against all this must be set the lessening of strain on those who worked in the heavy trades, and the decline in the number of crippled and deformed people that followed the introduction of power in places like Sheffield. There must be set, also, the reduction of sweating of women and young children, the rise in family earnings, the greater regularity of pay, and the gain in welfare that came as industrial work was taken out of the home.

Whether the houses themselves were becoming better or worse is diffi-cult to determine: much depends on the periods compared. Many of the dwellings provided for the workers by the country factory masters have survived—at Cromford, Mellor, and Styal. They have design and proportion, and, even by modern standards, are not wanting in amenity and comfort. But these were put up when building materials were plentiful, wages relatively low, and money relatively cheap. After 1793 the import of timber from the Baltic was restricted, and the price of labour of bricklayers and carpenters went up. At least two-thirds of the rent of a dwelling consists of interest charges: rates of interest were rising, and for more than a generation they remained high. This meant that if dwellings were to be let at rents which the workers could afford to pay they had to be smaller and less durable than those of the 'eighties. The rows of ill-built, back-to-back houses, into which the rapidly growing population of the towns was pressed, were largely the product of wartime conditions.

After 1815 matters were made worse by the influx of Irish, who, gregar-ious by instinct, crowded into the seaports and the towns of the North. Careful estimates made by members of the Manchester Statistical Society in the middle 'thirties led to the conclusion that about one-sixth of the families in Manchester were Irish, and that the percentage of the people living in cellars was 11.75. In Liverpool, where again there were many Irish, no less than 15 per cent of the inhabitants were in cellars. But in the newer towns, which were the special creation of the industrial revolution, conditions were far less grim. In Bury, where there were few Irish (and few hand-loom weavers) only 3.75 per cent, and in Ashton-under-Lyne only 1.25 per cent, of the people were housed in this way. In these places, the investigators re-ported, the houses of the workers were not only less crowded, but also better furnished and cleaner than those of the cities.

An historian has written of "the disasters of the industrial revolution." If by this he means that the years 1760–1830 were darkened by wars and made cheerless by dearth, no objection can be made to the phrase. But if he means that the technical and economic changes were themselves the source of calamity the opinion is surely perverse. The central problem of the age was how to feed and clothe and employ generations of children outnumbering by far those of any earlier time. Ireland was faced by the same problem. Failing to solve it, she lost in the 'forties about a fifth of her people by emigration or starvation and disease. If England had remained a nation of cultivators and craftsmen, she could hardly have escaped the same fate, and, at best, the weight of a growing population must have pressed down the spring of her spirit. She was delivered, not by her rulers, but by those who, seeking no doubt their own narrow ends, had the wit and resource to devise new instruments of production and new methods of administering industry. There are to-day on the plains of India and China men and women, plague-ridden and hungry, living lives little better, to outward appearance, than those of the cattle that toil with them by day and share their places of sleep by night. Such Asiatic standards, and such unmechanized horrors, are the lot of those who increase their numbers without passing through an industrial revolution.